60* Quick Baby Knits

BLANKETS, BOOTIES,
SWEATERS & MORE IN
CASCADE 220™
SUPERWASH

*

sixth&spring books

sixth&spring books

161 Avenue of the Americas, New York, New York 10013
sixthandspringbooks.com

Managing Editor
WENDY WILLIAMS

Senior Editor
MICHELLE BREDESON

Art Director
DIANE LAMPHRON

Yarn Editor
RENEE LORION

Instructions Editors
PAT HARSTE
EVE NG

Instructions Proofreader
JUDY SLOAN

Technical Illustrations
ULI MONCH

Page Layout
MICHELLE HENNING

Model Photography
DAN HOWELL

Still-Life Photography
JACK DEUTSCH

Fashion and Prop Stylists
SARAH LIEBOWITZ
BECCA LOEWENBERG

Vice President, Publisher
TRISHA MALCOLM

Creative Director
JOE VIOR

Production Manager
DAVID JOINNIDES

President
ART JOINNIDES

Library of Congress Control Number: 2010942325
ISBN: 978-1-936096-13-8
Manufactured in China
5 7 9 10 8 6

cascadeyarns.com

Introduction

Following the success of *60 Quick Knits*, we are proud to present *60 Quick Baby Knits*—a colorful collection of all-new patterns for newborns to toddlers.

We received such a positive response to our pint-sized patterns in *60 Quick Knits* that we knew knitters were craving more designs for little ones. All of the projects in this book are knit in 220 Superwash®, the perfect yarn for baby knits. It's durable yet gentle to the touch. 220 Superwash yarn is, of course, ideal for babies and for the busy parents caring for them, and the huge range of colors will delight knitters, parents and other gift recipients, and most importantly, the babies and tots wearing them.

Whether you're knitting for your own little gal or guy or for a friend or loved one, you'll find dozens of irresistible projects, including:

✳ Cuddly blankets featuring a variety of stitch and color patterns

✳ Sweet lacy and embroidered booties

✳ Rugged hoodies and pullovers for rough-and-tumble tots

✳ Fair Isle and striped legwarmers

✳ A vintage-style striped cardigan trimmed with lace and other pretty toppers

✳ Graphic pattern hats to keep tiny ears warm and cozy

There is truly something for every knitter—and every baby—in this adorable collection.

To locate retailers that carry 220 Superwash, visit cascadeyarns.com.

Check It Out!

Turn to the inside back cover to find abbreviations, an explanation of skill levels, illustrations of embroidery stitches and even a handy ruler!

contents

Flower Stitch Booties

Tiny embroidered flowers adorn the toes of these nature-inspired slippers.
Make a pair for your little flower girl!

DESIGNED BY ANGELA JUERGENS

Size
Instructions are written for size 6 months.

Knitted measurements
Length of sole 4¼"/11cm
Width of foot 2¼"/6cm

Materials
■ 1 3½oz/100g ball (approx 220yd/201m) of Cascade Yarns *220 Superwash* (superwash wool) each in #906 chartreuse (MC) and #914A tahitian rose (CC)

■ Size 4 (3.5mm) circular needle, 24"/61cm length *or size to obtain gauge*

■ Size B-1 (2.25mm) crochet hook

■ Two ⅝"/16mm buttons

■ Tapestry needle

Note Booties are made in one piece, including straps.

Stitch glossary
kf&b Inc 1 by knitting into the front and back of the next st.

M1 Insert LH needle from back to front under the strand between last st worked and the next st on the LH needle. Knit into the front loop to twist the st.

Seed stitch
(over an odd number of sts)

Row 1 K1, *p1, k1; rep from * to end.
Row 2 K the purl sts and p the knit sts.
Rep row 2 for seed st.

Left bootie
Beg at sole, with MC, cast on 35 sts using long-tail cast-on method. Do *not* join. Work back and forth as foll:
Row 1 (WS) Knit.

BOTTOM OF HEEL AND TOE SHAPING
Row 2 (RS) Kf&b, k16, M1, k1, M1, k16, kf&b—39 sts. **Row 3** Knit. **Row 4** Kf&b, k17, M1, k3, M1, k17, kf&b—43 sts. **Row 5** Knit. **Row 6** Kf&b, k18, M1, k1, M1, k3, M1, k1, M1, k18, kf&b—49 sts. **Row 7** Knit. **Row 8** Kf&b, k19, M1, k1, M1, k7, M1, k1, M1, k19, kf&b—55 sts. **Rows 9 and 10** Knit. **Rows 11–21** Work in seed st.

TOP OF TOE SHAPING
Row 22 K17, [ssk] 5 times, k1, [k2tog] 5 times, k17—45 sts.
Rows 23 and 24 Knit.

TOP OF TOE OPENING
Row 25 (WS) K11, bind off next 23 sts very tightly to gather edge, knit to end—11 sts each side of bound-off sts. Turn piece to RS. Slide 11 sts from left half of bootie to tip of RH needle, then transfer these sts to the LH needle. Side edges of bootie that form the center back seam now meet. Cut yarn, leaving long tail for sewing.

STRAP
Next row Cast on 13 sts to RH needle using backward loop cast-on method. Knit first 10 sts of bootie, k2tog to connect sides, knit last 10 sts—34 sts. Knit every row for 5 rows. Bind off knitwise. Cut yarn, leaving 10"/25.5cm tail for crocheted button loop; do not draw yarn through rem st.

BUTTON LOOP
Place rem st on crochet hook, tightly ch 5. Fasten off; do not cut yarn. Use tail to sew end of ch to opposite corner of strap. Use MC tail to sew center back seam and sole seam.

Right bootie
Work same as left bootie to strap.

STRAP
Next row Knit first 10 sts of bootie, k2tog to connect sides, knit last 10 sts, then cast on 13 sts using backward loop cast-on method—34 sts. Work strap same as for left bootie.

Finishing
Using CC, embroider three evenly spaced 5-petal lazy-daisy stitch flowers on front of each toe. Using CC, embroider French knot in center of each flower. Sew on buttons. ■

Gauge
24 sts and 32 rows to 4"/10cm over seed st using size 4 (3.5mm) circular needle. *Take time to check gauge.*

Sheep Hat

Little Bo-Peep won't lose her charge when
it's part of this cute-as-can-be cap.

DESIGNED BY RENEE LORION

Size
Instructions are written for
size 6–12 months.

Knitted measurements
Head circumference 16"/40.5cm
Depth 7"/17.5cm

Materials
■ 1 3½oz/100g ball (approx 220yd/
201m) of Cascade Yarns *220
Superwash* (superwash wool) each in
#910A winter white (MC),
#906 chartreuse (A) and #862
walnut heather (B)

■ One set (5) size 6 (4mm)
double-pointed needles (dpns)
or size to obtain gauge

■ 12"/30.5cm of DK or worsted weight
yarn in black (for eyes)

■ Stitch marker

■ Tapestry needle

Stitch glossary
M1 Insert LH needle from back to front
under the strand between last st worked
and the next st on the LH needle. Knit
into the front loop to twist the st.

Trinity stitch
(over a multiple of 4 sts)
Rnd 1 Purl.
Rnd 2 *(K1, p1, k1) in next st, p3tog; rep
from * around.
Rnd 3 Purl.
Rnd 4 *P3tog. (K1, p1, k1) in next st; rep
from * around.
Rep rnds 1–4 for trinity st.

Hat
With A, cast on 84 sts, dividing sts evenly
over 4 needles. Join and pm, taking care
not to twist sts on needles.
Purl next 2 rnds.

LEGS
Note Use a separate strand of B for each
pair of legs. Strand the yarn back and
forth between the legs.
Next rnd K14 with A, k4 with B, k6 with
A, k4 with B, k28 with A, k4 with B, k6
with A, k4 with B, k14 with A. Rep this
rnd 6 times more. Cut A and B. Change
to MC. Knit next rnd. Cont in trinity st
and rep rnds 1–4 five times.

CROWN SHAPING
Dec rnd 1 *P2tog p5; rep from *
around—72 sts.
Next rnd Work rnd 2 of trinity st.
Dec rnd 2 *P2tog, p7; rep from *
around—64 sts.
Next rnd Work rnd 4 of trinity st.
Dec rnd 3 *P2tog, p6; rep from *
around—56 sts.
Next rnd Work rnd 2 of trinity st.

Gauge
21 sts and 24 rnds to 4"/10cm over trinity st using size 6 (4mm) dpns.
Take time to check gauge.

Dec rnd 4 *P2tog, p5; rep from * around—48 sts.
Next rnd Work rnd 4 of trinity st.
Dec rnd 5 *P2tog, p2; rep from * around—36 sts.
Next rnd Work rnd 2 of trinity st.
Dec rnd 6 *[P2tog] 8 times, p2; rep from * around once more—20 sts.
Next rnd Work rnd 4 of trinity st.
Dec rnd 7 [P2tog] 10 times—10 sts.
Cut yarn, leaving an 8"/20.5cm tail and thread through rem sts. Pull tog tightly and secure end.

Finishing
HEAD
Beg at bottom edge, with dpn and B, cast on 7 sts. Work back and forth on two dpns as foll:
Row 1 and all WS rows Purl.
Row 2 (RS) K1, M1, knit to last st, M1, k1—9 sts.
Row 4 Rep row 2—11 sts.
Row 6 Rep row 2—13 sts.
Row 8 Rep row 2—15 sts.
Rows 10, 12 and 14 Knit.
Row 16 K1, ssk, knit to last 3 sts, k2tog, k1—13 sts.
Row 18 Rep row 16—11 sts.
Row 20 Rep row 16—9 sts.
Bind off all sts purlwise.

EARS (make 2)
Beg at bottom edge, with dpn and B, cast on 1 st. Work back and forth on two dpns as foll:
Row 1 (WS) Purl.
Row 2 (RS) (K1, p1, k1) in st—3 sts.
Row 3 Purl.
Row 4 K1, (k1, p1, k1) in next st, k1—5 sts.
Row 5 Purl.
Row 6 K2tog, k1, k2tog—3 sts.
Row 7 Purl.
Row 8 K3tog—1 st. Fasten off last st.

TAIL
Beg at bottom edge, with dpn and B, cast on 1 st. Work back and forth on two dpns as foll:
Row 1 (RS) [K1, p1] twice in st, k1 in same st—5 sts.
Row 2 P1, M1 p-st, purl to last st, M1 p-st, p1—7 sts.
Rows 3 and 5 Knit.
Row 4 Purl.
Row 6 [P1, p2tog] twice, p1—5 sts.
Row 7 K2tog, k1, k2tog—3 sts.
Row 8 P3tog—1 st. Fasten off last st.

ASSEMBLING
Using B, sew head to front of hat so bottom edge is 2½"/6.5cm from bottom edge of hat and centered between front legs. Sew on ears. Using black yarn, embroider French knot eyes. Using B, sew tail to back of hat so bottom edge is 2¾"/7cm from bottom edge of hat and centered between back legs. ■

Sporty Cardigan

Change the colors of the peppy stripes to easily customize this hoodie for a favorite school or team.

DESIGNED BY VERONICA MANNO

INTERMEDIATE

Sizes

Instructions are written for size 6 months. Changes for 12 and 18 months are in parentheses.

Knitted measurements

Chest (closed) 22 (24, 26)"/56 (61,66)cm
Length 11¼ (12¼, 13¼)"/28.5 (31, 33.5)cm
Upper arm 8 (9, 10)"/20.5 (23, 25.5)cm

Materials

■ 1 (1, 2) 3½oz/100g balls (each approx 220yd/201m) of Cascade Yarns *220 Superwash* (superwash wool) each in #1925 cobalt heather (A), #871 white (B) and #906 chartreuse (C)

■ Sizes 6 and 7 (4 and 4.5mm) circular needles, 32"/81cm length *or size to obtain gauge*

■ One pair each sizes 6 and 7 (4 and 4.5mm) needles

■ Stitch holders

■ Four ¹⁵/₁₆"/24mm buttons

Note

Body is worked in one piece to the underarms.

K2, p2 rib

(over a multiple of 4 sts plus 2)
Row 1 (RS) K2, *p2, k2;
rep from * to end.
Row 2 P2, *k2, p2; rep from * to end.
Rep rows 1 and 2 for k2, p2 rib.

Stripe pattern

Working in St st, *work 8 rows B, 8 rows C; rep from * (16 rows) for stripe pat.

Body

With smaller circular needle and A, cast on 102 (114, 122) sts. Work in k2, p2 rib for 10 rows. Inc 3 sts evenly across last row—105 (117, 125). Change to larger circular needle and B. Cont in St st (knit on RS, purl on WS) and stripe pat until 4 (5, 5) stripes have been completed, end with a WS row. With next color, work even for 7 (3, 7) rows, end with a RS row.

DIVIDE FOR FRONTS AND BACK

Next row (WS) P 21 (24, 26) sts, place these sts on holder for left front, bind off next 6 sts for left underarm, purl until there are 51 (57, 61) sts on RH needle,

leave these sts on needle for back, bind off next 6 sts for right underarm, purl to end, place these last 21 (24, 26) sts on holder for right front.

Back

Change to larger straight needles. Cont in stripe pat and work as foll:

ARMHOLE SHAPING
Bind off 2 sts at beg of next 2 rows. Dec 1 st each side on next row, then every other row 1 (2, 3) times more—43 (47, 49) sts. Work even until armhole measures 4 (4½, 5)"/10 (11.5, 12.5)cm, end with a WS row. Bind off.

Left front

Place 21 (24, 26) sts from left front holder onto larger straight needle ready for a RS row. Cont in stripe pat and work as foll:

ARMHOLE SHAPING
Bind off 2 sts at beg of next row. Work next row even. Dec 1 st from armhole edge on next row, then every other row 1 (2, 3) times more—17 (19, 20) sts. Work even until armhole measures 2½ (3, 3½)"/6.5 (7.5, 9)cm, end with a RS row.

Gauge

21 sts and 28 rows to 4"/10cm over St st using larger circular needle.
Take time to check gauge.

Sporty Cardigan

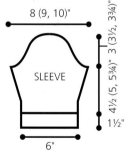

NECK SHAPING
Bind off 5 sts from neck edge once, 2 sts once, then 1 st once—9 (11, 12) sts. Work even until piece measures same length at back to shoulder, end with a WS row. Bind off.

RIGHT FRONT
Place 21 (24, 26) sts from right front holder onto larger straight needle ready for a RS row. Cont to work in stripe pat, work next row even. Cont to work same as left front, reversing shaping.

Sleeves
With smaller straight needles and A, cast on 34 sts. Work in k2, p2 rib for 10 rows, end with a WS row. Change to larger straight needles and C. Beg with a C stripe, cont in St st and stripe pat. Inc 1 st each side on next row, then every 4th row 4 (6, 8) times more—44 (48, 52) sts. AT THE SAME TIME, when 3 (4, 4) stripes have been completed, end with a WS row. Change to next color and work for 6 (2, 6) rows; piece should measure approx 5¾ (6¼, 7)"/14.5 (16, 18)cm from beg.

CAP SHAPING
Bind off 3 sts at beg of next 2 rows, then 2 sts at beg of next 2 rows. Dec 1 st from each side on next row, then every other row 3 (4, 5) times more, then every 4th row twice. Bind off 4 sts at beg of next 4 rows. Bind off rem 6 (8, 10) sts.

Hood
With larger straight needles and C, cast on 80 (84, 88) sts. Cont in St st and stripe pat and work even until 5 stripes have been completed. Bind off.

Finishing
Block pieces to measurements. Sew shoulder seams. Fold hood in half, then sew cast-on edges tog for back seam. Sew hood to neck edge, placing back seam in center of back neck edge. Place markers for 4 buttons on left front edge for girls and right front edge for boys, with the first ¾"/2cm from lower edge, the last 1½"/4cm from neck edge and the others evenly spaced between.

OUTER BAND
With RS facing, smaller circular needle and A, pick up and k 53 (59, 63) sts evenly spaced along right front edge to hood, pick up and k 80 (84, 88) sts along hood edge, pick up and k 53 (59, 63) sts evenly spaced along left front edge—186 (202, 214) sts. Beg with row 2, cont in k2, p2 rib for 3 rows.

Next (buttonhole) row (RS) *Work in rib to marker, bind off next 2 sts; rep from * 3 times more, work in rib to end.

Next row Work in rib, casting on 2 sts over bound-off sts. Cont in rib for 3 rows more. Bind off loosely in rib. Sew sleeve seams, matching stripes. Set in sleeves, matching stripes. Sew on buttons. ∎

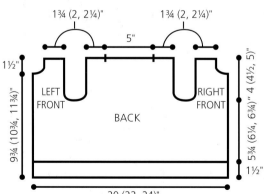

8 (9, 10)"

3 (3½, 3¾)"

SLEEVE

4½ (5, 5¾)"

1½"

6"

1¾ (2, 2¼)"   1¾ (2, 2¼)"

5"

1½"

9¾ (10¾, 11¾)"

LEFT FRONT   RIGHT FRONT

BACK

5¾ (6¼, 6¾)"   4 (4½, 5)"

1½"

20 (22, 24)"

Smocked Dress

Knitted smocking on the bodice gives this jumper
frock a sweetly old-fashioned feel.

DESIGNED BY AMY POLCYN

Sizes

Instructions are written for size 12 months.
Changes for 18 and 24 months are in
parentheses.

Knitted measurements

Chest (unstretched) 17 (19½, 20½)"/43
(49.5, 52)cm
Skirt 25 (28, 30)"/63.5 (71, 76)cm
Length (excluding straps) 13 (14, 15)"/33
(35.5, 38)cm

Materials

■ 2 (3, 3) 3½oz/100g balls (each
approx 220yd/201m) of Cascade Yarns *220
Superwash Quatro* (superwash wool) in
#1934 pink haze

■ Size 7 (4.5mm) circular needle, 24"/61cm
length *or size to obtain gauge*

■ One pair size 7 (4.5mm) needles

■ Stitch marker

■ Two 1"/25mm buttons

Note Skirt and bodice are made in one
piece from the bottom edge up.

Stitch glossary

Smocking st Insert RH needle from front
between 6th and 7th sts on LH needle and
draw through a loop; sl this loop onto

LH needle and k tog with the first st
on LH needle.

Smocking stitch

(over a multiple of 8 sts)
Rnds 1, 2 and 3 *K2, p2; rep from
* around. **Rnd 4** *Smocking st, k1, p2, k2,
p2; rep from * around. **Rnds 5, 6 and 7**
*K2, p2; rep from * around.
Rnd 8 K2, p2, *smocking st, k1, p2, k2,
p2; rep from * around, end last rep
work smocking st between 2nd and 3rd
sts at beg of next rnd to complete last
smocking st; do not move marker.
Rep rnds 1–8 for smocking st.

Dress

SKIRT
With circular needle, cast on 120 (136,
144) sts. Join and pm for beg of rnds.
Work around in k2, p2 rib for 1½"/4cm.
Cont in St st (knit every rnd) until piece
measures 9 (10, 11)"/23 (25.5, 28)cm.

BODICE
Work in smocking st for 4"/10cm, end
with rnd 2 or 6. Bind off in rib.

Straps (make 2)

With straight needles, cast on 10 sts.
Row 1 (RS) K2, *p2, k2; rep from *to end.
Row 2 P2, *k2, p2; rep from * to end.

Rep rows 1 and 2 until piece measures 8
(8½, 9)"/20.5 (21.5, 23)cm from beg, end
with a WS row.

Next (buttonhole) row (RS) Work in rib
over first 3 sts, bind off next 4 sts,
work in rib to end. **Next row** Work in rib,
casting on 4 sts over bound-off sts.
Cont to work even for 4 rows. **Dec row 1
(RS)** Ssk, work in rib to last 2 sts, k2tog.
Dec row 2 P2tog tbl, work in rib to
last 2 sts, p2tog. Bind off rem 6 sts in rib.

Finishing

Lightly block piece to measurements.
For each strap, work as foll:
On WS of bodice back, position cast-on
edge 1"/2.5cm below top edge of bodice
and so outside edge of strap is approx 1¼
(1½, 1½)"/3 (4, 4)cm from side edge of
bodice. Sew in place. Sew on buttons. ■

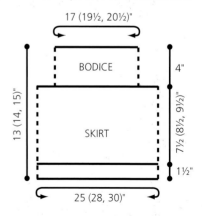

Gauges

24 sts and 31 rnds to 5"/12.5cm over St st using size 7 (4.5mm) circular needle.
28 sts and 24 rnds to 4"/10cm over smocking st using size 7 (4.5mm) circular needle. *Take time to check gauges.*

Fan Stitch Blanket

This striking nature-inspired pattern makes for a stunning single-color throw.

DESIGNED BY JACQUELINE VAN DILLEN

EXPERIENCED

Knitted measurements
Approx 28" x 31½"/71cm x 80cm

Materials
■ 5 3½oz/100g balls (each approx 220yd/201m) of Cascade Yarns *220 Superwash* (superwash wool) in #1914 alaska sky

■ Size 6 (4mm) circular needle, 36"/ 91cm length *or size to obtain gauge*

■ Stitch markers

Blanket
Cast on 133 sts. Work in garter st (knit every row) for 10 rows, end with a WS row.

BEG CHART PAT
Row 1 (RS) K6, pm, work st 1, work 20-st rep 6 times, pm, k6.
Row 2 K6, sl marker, work 20-st rep 6 times, work st 1, sl marker, k6.
Keeping 6 sts each side in garter st, cont to foll chart in this way to row 34, then rep rows 3–34 five times more, then rows 3–18 once.
Cont in garter st for 10 rows. Bind off all sts knitwise.

Finishing
Block piece lightly to measurements. ■

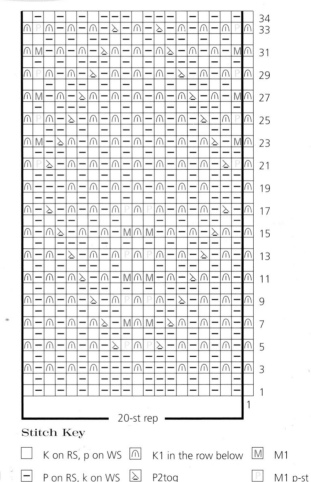

20-st rep

Stitch Key

☐ K on RS, p on WS	⋒ K1 in the row below	Ⓜ M1
⊟ P on RS, k on WS	⊠ P2tog	M1 p-st

Gauge
19 sts and 30 rows to 4"/10cm over chart pat using size 6 (4mm) circular needle. *Take time to check gauge.*

6

Striped Hat and Bootie Set

A spirited set of colorful accessories is perfect for a day out and about in the stroller.

DESIGNED BY ERSSIE MAJOR

Size
Instructions are written for size newborn–3 months.

Knitted measurements

HAT
Head circumference 14½"/37cm
Depth 6"/15cm

BOOTIES
Foot circumference 4½"/11.5cm
Foot length 4½"/11.5cm

Materials
■ 1 3½oz/100g ball (approx 220yd /201m) of Cascade Yarns *220 Superwash* (superwash wool) each in #840 iris (MC) and #910A winter white (CC)

HAT
■ Size 7 (4.5mm) circular needle, 16"/40cm length *or size to obtain gauge*

■ One set (5) size 7 (4.5mm) double-pointed needles (dpns)

■ Stitch holder

■ Stitch markers

BOOTIES
■ One set (5) size 6 (4mm) double-pointed needles (dpns) *or size to obtain gauge*

■ Stitch holder

■ Stitch markers

K2, p2 rib
(multiple of 4 sts)
Rnd 1 (RS) *K2, p2; rep from * around.
Rep rnd 1 or k2, p2 rib.

Stripe pattern
Working in St st, *work 2 rnds CC, 2 rnds MC; rep from * (4 rnds) for stripe pat
.

Short row wrap & turn (w&t)
On RS row (on WS row):
1) Wyib (wyif), sl next st purlwise.
2) Move yarn between the needles to the front (back).
3) Sl the same st back to LH needle. Turn work. One st is wrapped.
4) When working the wrapped st, insert RH needle under the wrap and work it tog with the corresponding st on needle.

Hat
With circular needle and MC, cast on 72 sts. Join and pm for beg of rnds. Purl 1 rnds. Work in k2, p2 rib for 10 rnds. Cont in St st (knit every rnd) and stripe pat until piece measures 5"/12.5cm from beg, end with 2 rnds CC. Cont in stripe pat and work as foll:

CROWN SHAPING
Note Change to dpns (dividing sts evenly between 4 needles) when there are too few sts to work with circular needle.
Dec rnd 1 *K7, k2tog; rep from * around—64 sts.
Dec rnd 2 *K6, k2tog; rep from * around—56 sts.
Dec rnd 3 *K5, k2tog; rep from * around—48 sts.
Dec rnd 4 *K4, k2tog; rep from * around—40 sts.
Cut CC and work with MC only.
Dec rnd 5 *K3, k2tog; rep from * around—32 sts.
Dec rnd 6 *K2, k2tog; rep from * around—24 sts.
Dec rnd 7 *K1, k2tog; rep from * around—16 sts.
Dec rnd 8 [K2tog] 8 times—8 sts.
Leave first 4 sts on dpn for first I-cord, place rem 4 sts on holder for 2nd I-cord.

Gauges
HAT 20 sts and 26 rnds to 4"/10cm over St st using size 7 (4.5mm) circular needle.
BOOTIES 22 sts and 32 rnds to 4"/10cm over St st using size 6 (4mm) dpns.
Take time to check gauges.

Striped Hat and Bootie Set

I-CORDS

Work in I-cord (see page 20) as foll:
*Next row (RS) With 2nd dpn, k4, do not turn. Slide sts back to beg of needle to work next row from RS; rep from * until I-cord measures 9"/23cm from beg. Cut yarn, leaving a 6"/15cm tail and thread through rem sts. Pull tog tightly and secure end. Place 4 sts from holder back on dpn. With CC, work same as first I-cord. Tie I-cords in a bow for a girl, or knot together for a boy.

Right bootie
CUFF

With dpn and MC, cast on 24 sts. Divide sts over 4 needles (6 sts on each). Join, taking care not to twist sts on needles, pm for beg of rnds. Beg of rnds will be on the inside of the leg and foot. Work around in k2, p2 rib for 24 rnds. Cont in St st (knit every rnd) and beg stripe pat as foll: 2 rnds CC, 2 rnds MC, 2 rnds CC and 1 rnd MC.

BEG HEEL FLAP

Note Heel flap is worked back and forth on one dpn over half the sts. Place 6 sts each from Needle 1 and Needle 2 on one dpn; dropping marker, set aside sts on Needles 3 and 4.
****With MC only, work short row shaping as foll:
Row 1 Knit to last st, w&t.
Row 2 Purl to last st, w&t.
Row 3 Knit to last unwrapped st, w&t.
Row 4 Purl to last unwrapped st, w&t.

Rep rows 3 and 4 until 4 sts have been wrapped each side of the heel, leaving 4 sts unwrapped in the center. Pick up and work wraps as foll:
Row 1 Knit to first wrapped st, pick up wrap(s) and knit wrap(s) and st tog, then w&t around next st (which will now be wrapped twice. Pick up both wraps and knit tog with st when you come to them as you cont to work rows).
Row 2 Purl to first wrapped st, pick up wrap(s) and purl wrap(s) and st tog tbl, then w&t around next st (which will now be wrapped twice. Pick up both wraps and purl tog tbl with st when you come to them as you cont to work rows). Rep these 2 rows until all wraps and sts have been worked, end with a RS row.** To resume working in the rnd, knit across sts on Needles 3 and 4. Place 6 sts each back onto Needle 1 and Needle 2. Pm for beg of rnds between Needle 1 and Needle 4.

FOOT

Beg with 2 rnds CC, cont in stripe pat until foot measures 3¾"/9.5cm from back of heel, end with 2 rnds MC. Cont with MC only as foll:

TOE

Place 6 sts each from Needle 1 and Needle 2 on one dpn (now Needle 1), then place rem 12 sts from Needle 3 and Needle 4 on a 2nd dpn (now Needle 2). With 3rd dpn, cont as foll:
Dec rnd 1 [K1, ssk, k6, k2tog, k1] twice—20 sts.

Dec rnd 2 [K1, ssk, k4, k2tog, k1] twice—16 sts.
Dec rnd 3 [K1, ssk, k2, k2tog, k1] twice—12 sts. Graft 6 sts on Needle 1 and 6 sts on Needle 2 tog using Kitchener stitch.

Left bootie
CUFF

With dpn and MC, cast on 24 sts. Divide sts over 4 needles (6 sts on each). Join, taking care not to twist sts on needles, pm for beg of rnds. Beg of rnds will be on the inside of the leg and foot. Work around in k2, p2 rib for 24 rnds. Cont in St st (knit every rnd) and beg stripe pat as foll: 2 rnds CC, 2 rnds MC, 2 rnds CC.
Next rnd With MC, knit to Needle 3.

BEG HEEL FLAP

Note Heel flap is worked back and forth on one dpn over half the sts. Place 6 sts from Needle 3 onto Needle 4; dropping marker, set aside sts on Needles 1 and 2. Rep from ** to ** same as right bootie. To resume working in the rnd, knit across sts on Needles 1 and 2 and first 6 sts on heel flap dpn (this is again Needle 3. Rem 6 sts on heel flap dpn is again Needle 4). Pm for beg of rnds between Needle 1 and Needle 4.

FOOT

Work same as for right bootie.

TOE

Work same as for right bootie. ■

To make I-cord, cast on anywhere from 3 to 5 stitches, *knit, do not turn. Slip the stitches back to the beginning of the row. Pull the yarn tightly from the end of the row Repeat from * until the I-cord is as long as desired. Bind off.

Garter Stitch Cardigan

Reminiscent of a Chanel design, this classy little sweater will never go out of style.

DESIGNED BY BRANDY FORTUNE

INTERMEDIATE

Sizes
Instructions are written for size 6 months. Changes for 12 and 18 months are in parentheses.

Knitted measurements
Chest (closed) 22 (24, 26)"/56 (61, 66)cm
Length 9½ (10½, 11½)"/24 (26.5, 29)cm
Upper arm 7 (8, 9)"/18 (20.5, 23)cm

Materials
■ 2 (3, 3) 3½oz/100g balls (each approx 220yd/201m) of Cascade Yarns *220 Superwash* (superwash wool) in #1941 salmon (MC)

■ 1 ball in #874 ridge rock (CC)

■ Size 6 (4mm) circular needle, 32"/81cm length *or size to obtain gauge*

■ One set (5) size 6 (4mm) double-pointed needles (dpns)

■ Stitch holders

■ Stitch markers

■ One ¾"/19mm button

Notes
1) Yoke and body are worked back and forth in one piece from the neck down.
2) Sleeves are worked in the round.

Stitch glossary
kf&b Inc 1 by knitting into the front and back of the next st.

Border stripe
Rows 1 and 2 With CC, knit.
Rows 3 and 4 With MC, knit.
Rows 5 and 6 With CC, knit.
Rows 7 and 8 With MC, knit.
Row 9 With CC, knit.
Work rows 1–9 for border stripe.

Gauge
20 sts and 42 rows to 4"/10cm over St st using size 6 (4mm) circular needle.
Take time to check gauge.

Garter Stitch Cardigan

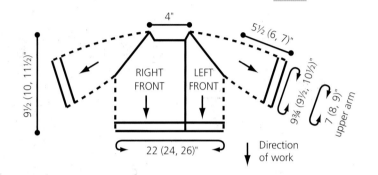

Rep inc rnd every 12th rnd 3 times more—44 (48, 54) sts. Work even until piece measures 4½ (5, 6)"/11.5 (12.5, 15)cm from beg, end with a purl rnd. Work around in border stripe as foll:
Rnd 1 With CC, knit.
Rnd 2 With CC, purl.
Rnd 3 With MC, knit.
Rnd 4 With MC, purl.
Rnd 5 With CC, knit.
Rnd 6 With CC, purl.
Rnd 7 With MC, knit.
Rnd 8 With MC, purl.
Rnd 9 With CC, knit. Bind off purlwise.

Finishing
Block piece to measurements.

RIGHT FRONT BAND
With RS facing, circular needle and CC, pick up and k 45 (50, 55) sts evenly spaced along right front edge. Work rows 2–9 of border stripe, end with a RS row. With CC, bind off all sts knitwise.

LEFT FRONT BAND
Work same as right front band.

NECKBAND
With RS facing, circular needle and CC, pick up and k 45 sts evenly spaced along entire neck edge. Work rows 2–4 of border stripe, end with a WS row.
Row (buttonhole) 5 (RS) With CC, k3, yo, k2tog, knit to end. Work rows 6–9 of border stripe. With CC, bind off all sts knitwise. Sew on button. ■

Cardigan
YOKE
Beg at neck edge, with circular needle and MC, cast on 28 sts. Knit next row.
Inc row 1 (RS) Kf&b (left front), pm, [kf&b] twice (left sleeve), pm, kf&b, k20, kf&b (back), pm, [kf&b] twice (right sleeve), pm, kf&b (right front)—36 sts. Knit next row.
Inc row 2 (RS) Kf&b, *knit to 1 st before next marker, kf&b, sl marker, kf&b; rep from * 3 times more, knit to last st, end kf&b—46 sts. Knit next row. Rep last 2 rows 3 times more—76 sts.
Inc row 3 (RS) *Knit to 1 st before next marker, kf&b, sl marker, kf&b; rep from * 3 times more, then cast on 15 sts—99 sts. Knit next row.
Inc row 4 (RS) *Knit to 1 st before next marker, kf&b, sl marker, kf&b; rep from * 3 times more, knit to end. Knit next row. Rep last 2 rows 8 (10, 13) times more—171 (187, 211) sts. Cont to work even in garter st (knit every row) until piece measures 4 (4½, 5)"/10 (11.5, 12.5)cm from beg (measured from center back neck).

DIVIDE FOR BODY AND SLEEVES
Next row (RS) K 20 (22, 25) sts (left front), place next 32 (36, 42) sts on holder (left sleeve), cast on 4 sts (left underarm), k 52 (56, 62) sts (back), place next 32 (36, 42) sts on holder (right sleeve), cast on 4 sts (right underarm), k 35 (37, 40) sts (right front)—115 (123, 135) sts.

BODY
Cont in garter st until piece measures 7½ (8½, 9½)"/19 (21.5, 24)cm from beg (measured from center back neck), end with a WS row. Work rows 1–9 of border stripe, end with a RS row. With CC, bind off all sts knitwise.

SLEEVES
With RS facing, dpns and MC, skip first 2 sts of underarm cast-on, pick up and k 1 st in each of next 2 sts, k 32 (36, 42) sts from sleeve holder, pick up and k 1 st in each rem 2 sts of cast-on—36 (40, 46) sts. Divide sts evenly between 4 needles. Join and pm for beg of rnds. Purl next rnd. Work around in garter st (knit one rnd, purl one rnd), and work as foll:
Inc rnd Kf&b, knit to last st, kf&b.

Cable and Lace Blanket

Give the nursery a touch of sophistication with this afghan made up of twisting and eyelet columns and bordered by moss stitch.

DESIGNED BY LEE GANT

INTERMEDIATE

Sizes
Instructions are written for stroller blanket. Changes for crib blanket are in parentheses.

Finished measurements
Stroller blanket
Approx 25" x 30"/63.5cm x 76cm)
Crib blanket
Approx 32" x 40"/81cm x 101.5cm

Materials
- 3 (5) 3½oz/100g balls (each approx 220yd/200m) of Cascade Yarns *220 Superwash* (superwash wool) in #817 aran
- Size 7 (4.5mm) circular needle, 36"/91cm length *or size to obtain gauge*
- Cable needle (cn)
- Stitch markers

Stitch glossary
4-st LC Sl next 2 sts to cn and hold to *front*, k2, k2 from cn.

Seed stitch
(over any number of sts)
Row 1 (RS) *K1, p1; rep from * to end.
Row 2 K the purl sts and p the knit sts.
Rep row 2 for seed st.

Cable and lace stitch
(multiple of 10 sts plus 4)
Row 1 (RS) P1, k2tog, yo, *p2, k4, p2, k2tog, yo; rep from *, end p1.
Row 2 and all WS rows K1, p2, *k2, p4, k2, p2; rep from *, end k1.

Row 3 P1, yo, SKP, *p2, 4-st LC, p2, yo, SKP; rep from *, end p1.
Row 5 Rep row 1.
Row 7 P1, yo, SKP, *p2, k4, p2, yo, SKP; rep from *, end p1.
Row 8 Rep row 2.
Rep rows 1–8 for cable and lace st.

Blanket
Cast on 130 (170) sts. Work in seed st for 3"/7.5cm, end with a WS row.
Row 1 (RS) Work in seed st over first 13 sts, pm, work row 1 of cable and lace st to last 13 sts, pm, work in seed st over last 13 sts.
Row 2 Work in seed st to first marker, sl marker, work row 2 of cable and lace st to next marker, sl marker, work in seed st over last 13 sts. Keeping 13 sts each side in seed st, cont to work center 104 (144) sts in cable and lace st. Work even until piece measures 27 (37)"/68.5 (94)cm from beg, end with a WS row, dropping markers.
Work in seed st for 3"/7.5cm, end with a RS row. Bind off loosely in seed st.

Finishing
Block piece lightly to measurements. ■

Gauge
21 sts and 28 rows to 4"/10cm over cable and lace st using size 7 (4.5mm) circular needle (after blocking). *Take time to check gauge.*

Bolero Jacket

For when baby needs just a little cover-up, this crop top has a picot edging and lovely lace details.

DESIGNED BY HALLEH TEHRANIFAR

Sizes

Instructions are written for size 6 months. Changes for 12 and 18 months are in parentheses.

Knitted measurements

Chest 21 (22½, 24)"/53 (57,61)cm
Length 7½ (8, 9)"/19 (20, 23)cm

Materials

■ 2 (2, 2) 3½oz/100g balls (each approx 220yd/200m) of Cascade Yarns *220 Superwash* (superwash wool) in #837 berry pink

■ Size 5 (3.75mm) needles *or size to obtain gauge*

■ Size 7 (4.5mm) needles for edgings

■ Size 4 (3.5mm) double-pointed needles (dpns) and one ½"/13mm button for closure)

■ Stitch holders

Scallop edging

With RS facing, insert tip of needle into next loop/stitch.
Row 1 (RS) (K1, yo, k1) into same st—3 sts.
Row 2 P1, k in (front, back, front) of yo, p1—5 sts.

Row 3 Bind off all sts (1 st on needle), yo, insert tip of needle into next loop/stitch and k1—3 sts.
Rep rows 2 and 3 for edging, ending with bind-off on row 3—1 st.
Fasten off.

Back

With smaller needles, cast on 52 (56, 60) sts.
Work 8 (12, 14) rows in St st (k on RS, p on WS).
Work 2 rows of eyelet pat as foll:
Row 1 (RS) K3 (6, 4), *ssk, yo, k5; rep from * to last 0 (1, 0) st, k0 (1, 0).
Row 2 Purl.
Work 10 rows in St st.
Work butterfly eyelet pat as foll:
Rows 1 and 5 (RS) K6 (2, 7), *k2tog, yo, k1, yo, ssk, k2; rep from * to last 4 (5, 4) sts, k4 (5, 4).
Rows 2, 4 and 6 Purl.
Row 3 K7 (3, 8), *k2tog, yo, k5; rep from * to last 3 (4, 3) sts, k3 (4, 3).

ARMHOLE SHAPING

Cont in St st, bind off 4 (4, 5) sts at beg of next 2 rows, 2 sts at beg of next 2 rows—40 (44, 46) sts.
Work even in St st until armhole measures 3¼ (3½, 3¾)"/8.5 (9, 9.5)cm, ending with a WS row.

NECK SHAPING

Next row (RS) K17 (18, 19), join 2nd ball of yarn and bind off center 6 (8, 8) sts, k to end—17 (18, 19) sts each side. Working both sides at once, bind off 3 sts from each neck edge once. Place rem 14 (15, 16) sts each side on a holder.

Left front

With smaller needles, cast on 14 (14, 16) sts.
Row 1 (RS) K to last st, yo, k1.
Row 2 Sl 1, p to end.
Rep these 2 rows 3 (5, 6) times more—18 (20, 23) sts.
Work 2 rows of eyelet pat as foll:
Next row (RS) K4 (6, 9), k2tog, yo, k5, k2tog, yo, k4, yo, k1—19 (21, 24) sts.
Next row Sl 1, p to end.
Rep rows 1 and 2 five times—24 (26, 29) sts.
Work butterfly eyelet pat as foll:
Row 1 K7 (9, 12), k2tog, yo, k1, yo, ssk, k to last st, yo, k1—25 (27, 30) sts.
Row 2 Sl 1, p to end.
Row 3 K8 (9, 12), k2tog, yo, k to last st, yo, k1—26 (28, 31) sts.
Row 4 Sl 1, p to end.
Row 5 Rep row 1—27 (29, 32) sts.
Row 6 Sl 1, p to end.
Note Front increases are complete.

Gauge

20 sts and 27 rows to 4"/10cm over St st using smaller needles. *Take time to check gauge.*

Bolero Jacket

ARMHOLE SHAPING
Next row (RS) Bind off 4 (4, 5) sts, work to end.
Next row Purl.
Next row Bind off 2 sts, k to end—21 (23, 25) sts.
Work even in St st, slipping the first st on WS rows, until armhole measures 2¾ (3, 3¼)"/7 (7.5, 8.5)cm, end with a RS row.

NECK SHAPING
Row 1 (WS) Bind off 4 (5, 6) sts, p to end—17 (18, 19) sts.
Row 2 Knit.
Row 3 Bind off 3 sts, p to end—14 (15, 16) sts.
Work even until same length as back. Place sts on a holder.

Right front
With smaller needles, cast on 14 (14, 16) sts.
Row 1 (RS) Sl 1, yo, k to end.
Row 2 Purl.
Rep these 2 rows 3 (5, 6) times more—18 (20, 23) sts.
Work 2 rows of eyelet pat as foll:
Next row (RS) Sl 1, yo, k4, yo, ssk, k5, yo, ssk, k to end—19 (21, 24) sts.
Next row Purl.
Rep rows 1 and 2 five times—24 (26, 29) sts.
Work butterfly eyelet pat as foll:
Row 1 (RS) Sl 1, yo, k11, k2tog, yo, k1, yo, ssk, k to end—25 (27, 30) sts.
Row 2 Purl.
Row 3 Sl 1, yo, k14, yo, ssk, k to end—26 (28, 31) sts.

Row 4 Purl.
Row 5 (RS) Sl 1, yo, k13, k2tog, yo, k1, yo, ssk, k to end—27 (29, 32) sts.
Note Front increases are complete.

ARMHOLE SHAPING
Next row (WS) Bind off 4 (4, 5) sts, p to end.
Next row Knit.
Next row Bind off 2 sts, p to end—21 (23, 25) sts.
Work even in St st, slipping the first st on RS rows, until armhole measures 2¾ (3, 3¼)"/7 (7.5, 8.5)cm, ending with a WS row.

NECK SHAPING
Row 1 (RS) Bind off 4 (5, 6) sts, k to end—17 (18, 19) sts.
Row 2 Purl.
Row 3 Bind off 3 sts, k to end—14 (15, 16) sts.
Work even until same length as back. Place sts on a holder.

Sleeves
With smaller needles, cast on 28 (32, 34) sts.
Row 1 (RS) K1 (1, 2), *p2, k2; rep from * to last 3 (3, 4) sts, p2, k1 (1, 2).
Row 2 P1 (1, 2), *k2, p2; rep from * to last 3 (3, 4) sts, k2, p1 (1, 2).
Rep last 2 rows 7 times more.
Inc row (RS) K2 *yo, k4 (4, 3); rep from * to last 2 sts, yo, k2—35 (40, 45) sts.
Cont in St st until sleeve measures 4½ (5, 5½)"/11.5 (12.5, 14)cm from beg.
Inc row K1 (2, 3), *yo, k4; rep from * to last 2 sts, yo, k2—44 (50, 56) sts.
Cont in St st until sleeve measures 6 (7, 8)"/15 (18, 20.5)cm from beg.

CAP SHAPING
Bind off 4 (4, 5) sts at beg of next 2 rows.
Bind off 3 sts at beg of foll 2 rows.
Bind off rem 30 (36, 40) sts.

Finishing
Using 3-needle bind-off, join shoulder seams. Set sleeves into armholes, sewing from each side of underarm to ½"/1.5cm from shoulder seam. Fold extra fabric to inside to form pleat and sew in place to finish seam. Sew side and sleeve seams.

EDGINGS
Using larger needles, starting at right side seam, work scallop edging around entire front, neck and back edges. Starting at sleeve seam, work edging around each cuff. Join ends of edgings.

FRONT CLOSURE TAB
DISK (make 2)
Using dpns, cast on 3 sts and divide over 3 needles. Join for working in the round.
Rnd 1 [Kfb] 3 times—6 sts.
Rnd 2 [Kfb] 6 times—12 sts.
Bind off.
Place disks side by side and sew together to form tab. Sew one side of tab to top of scallop loop at right front neck. Sew button to WS of other side of tab. Use scallop loop on left front as buttonhole. ■

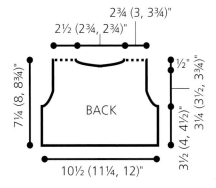

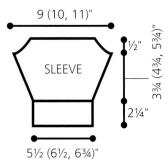

SLEEVE

9 (10, 11)"

½"

3¾ (4¾, 5¾)"

2¼"

5½ (6½, 6¾)"

BACK

2¾ (3, 3¾)"

2½ (2¾, 2¾)"

7¼ (8, 8¾)"

½"

3¼ (3½, 3¾)"

3½ (4, 4½)"

10½ (11¼, 12)"

LEFT FRONT

2¾ (3, 3¼)"

1½ (1½, 1¾)"

1"

6¼ (7, 7¾)"

2½ (2¾, 3)"   2¾ (2¾, 3¼)"

Quick Tip

The scalloped edge used here is a pretty and versatile one that can be added to any part of a finished project. Start from any point along the edge and adjust the tension according to your taste. Increase needle size to obtain larger scallops or pick up every stitch/loop on the edge of fabric for tighter scallops and more ruffles.

Leaf Lace Blanket

A delicate repeating openwork pattern gives this afghan a soft, light feel and makes it a perfect receiving piece for a newborn.

DESIGNED BY JOY SLAYTON

Knitted measurements

Approx 33" x 35"/84cm x 89cm

Materials

- 4 3½oz/100g balls (each approx 220yd/201m) of Cascade Yarns *220 Superwash* (superwash wool) in #1949 lavender
- Size 6 (4mm) circular needle, 36"/91cm length *or size to obtain gauge*
- Stitch markers

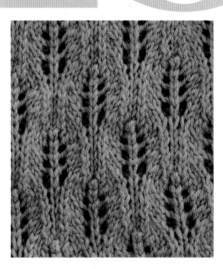

Leaf lace stitch

(over a multiple of 10 sts plus 1)
Row 1 (RS) K1, *yo, k2, k2tog, k1, ssk, k2, yo, k1; rep from * to end.
Row 2 and all WS rows Purl.
Rows 3, 5 and 7 Rep row 1.
Rows 9, 11, 13 and 15 K 1, *ssk, k2, yo, k1, yo, k2, k2tog, k1; rep from * to end.
Row 16 Rep row 2.
Rep rows 1–16 for leaf lace st.

Blanket

Cast on 143 sts.
Next row Sl 1 wyib, knit to end. Rep this row 4 times more.
Next (inc) row (RS) Sl 1 wyib, knit to end, inc 16 sts evenly spaced across—159 sts.
Set-up row (WS) Sl 1 wyib, k3, pm, purl to last 4 sts, pm, k4. Work in leaf lace pat st as foll:
Row 1 (RS) Sl 1 wyib, k3, sl marker, work in leaf lace st to next marker, sl marker, k4.
Row 2 Sl 1 wyib, k3, sl marker, work in leaf lace pat st to next marker, sl marker, k4. Keeping 4 sts each side as established, cont to work center 151 sts in leaf lace st to row 16, then rep rows 1–16 eleven times more, then rows 1–8 once, end with a WS row.
Next (dec) row (RS) Sl 1 wyib, knit to end, dec 16 sts evenly spaced across—143 sts.
Next row Sl 1 wyib, knit to end. Rep this row 4 times more. Bind off all sts knitwise.

Finishing

Block piece to measurements. ◼

Gauge

19 sts and 23 rows to 4"/10cm over leaf lace st using size 6 (4mm) circular needle (after blocking). *Take time to check gauge.*

Ruffled Cloche

This flapper-style hat has a pleated edge and a band of seed stitch "ribbon" topped off by an attached pink bow.

DESIGNED BY PAT OLSKI

INTERMEDIATE

Size
Instructions are written for size 6–12 months.

Knitted measurements
Head circumference 15"/38cm
Depth 7"/17.5cm

Materials
- 1 3½oz/100g ball (approx 220yd/ 200m) of Cascade Yarns *220 Superwash* (superwash wool) each in #910A winter white (MC), #1941 salmon (A) and #834 strawberry pink (B)
- One pair size 7 (4.5mm) needles *or size to obtain gauge*
- One set (5) size 7 (4.5mm) double-pointed needles (dpns)
- Stitch marker

Notes
1) The ruffle and seed st hatband are work in rows, then the piece is joined and worked in rnds.
2) When changing colors, pick up new color from under dropped color to prevent holes.
3) Keep all color changes on WS of work.

Hat
RUFFLE
With straight needles and MC, cast on 138 sts.
Row 1 (RS) K1, *p3, k5; rep from *, end k1.
Row 2 P1, *p5, k3; rep from *, end p1.
Row 3 Rep row 1.
Row (dec) 4 P1, *p5, ssk, k1; rep from *, end p1—121 sts.
Row 5 K1, *p2, k5; rep from *, end k1.
Row 6 P1, *p5, k2; rep from *, end p1.
Row (dec) 7 K1, *p2tog, k5; rep from *, end k1—104 sts.
Row 8 P1, *p5, k1; rep from *, end p1.
Row (dec) 9 K1, *k2tog, k4; rep from *, end k1—87 sts.
Row (dec) 10 Purl, dec 9 sts evenly spaced across—78 sts.
Row 11 (RS) Knit.

HATBAND
Work in seed st as foll:
Row 1 (WS) With A, p1, [k1, p1] 19 times, with B, k1, [p1, k1] 19 times.
Row 2 With B, k1, [p1, k1] 19 times, with A, p1, [k1, p1] 19 times.
Rep rows 1 and 2 five times more, then row 1 once, end with a WS row.

SIDES
Change to dpns, dividing sts evenly over 4 needles. **Next rnd** With MC, knit. Join and pm for beg of rnds. Cont to work in St st (knit every rnd) for 2"/5cm.

CROWN SHAPING
Next rnd *K13, pm; rep from * around 4 times more, end k13. Knit next rnd.
Dec rnd 1 K2tog, *knit to 2 st before next marker, ssk, sl marker, k2tog; rep from * around 4 times more, knit to last 2 sts, ssk—66 sts.
Knit next 2 rnds. Rep last 3 rnds 5 times more, dropping all but rnd marker on last dec rnd—6 sts. Cut yarn, leaving an 8"/20.5cm tail and thread through rem sts. Pull tog tightly and secure end.

Finishing
Using MC, sew ruffle seam, then using A, sew hatband seam.

BOW
With straight needles and A, cast on 8 sts, then with B, cast on 8 sts. Work in seed st as foll: **Row 1 (RS)** With B, [k1, p1] 4 times, with A, [k1, p1] 4 times.
Row 2 With A, [p1, k1] 4 times, with B, [p1, k1] 4 times. Rep rows 1 and 2 five times more, then row 1 once. Bind off each color in seed st. Thread B in tapestry needle. Sew running stitches along color change, then gather slightly to form bow shape. Center color change of bow over color change of hatband, so colors are reversed; as shown in photo. Using B, sew bow to hatband using straight stitches over color change. ■

Gauge
22 sts and 29 rows to 4"/10cm over St st using size 7 (4.5mm) needles.
Take time to check gauge.

Striped Blanket

Wide stockinette bands of pink and brown are framed in seed stitch, making this afghan a real room-brightener.

DESIGNED BY JEANNIE CHIN

EASY

Knitted measurements
Approx 29½" x 37"/75cm x 94cm

Materials
■ 4 3½oz/100g balls (each approx 220yd/201m) of Cascade Yarns *220 Superwash* (superwash wool) in #818 mocha (MC)

■ 2 balls in #840 iris (CC)

■ Size 6 (4mm) circular needle, 36"/91cm length *or size to obtain gauge*

Seed stitch
(over an even number of sts)
Row 1 (RS) *K1, p1; rep from * to end.
Row 2 K the purl sts and p the knit sts.
Rep row 2 for seed st.

Stripe pattern
Working in St st (knit on RS, purl on WS), *work 16 rows CC, 16 rows MC; rep from * (32 rows) for stripe pat.

Blanket
With CC, cast on 140 sts. Work in stripe pat, until 15 stripes have been completed, ending with a CC stripe. Bind off using CC.

SIDE BORDERS
With RS facing and MC, pick up and k 170 sts evenly along one side edge.
Next row (WS) Knit. Work in seed st for 2"/5cm, end with a WS row. Bind off in seed st. Rep for opposite side edge.

TOP BORDER
With RS facing and MC, pick up and k 11 sts along edge of side border, 140 sts along bound-off edge of blanket, then 11 sts along edge of side border —-162 sts.
Next row (WS) Knit. Work in seed st for 2"/5cm, end with a WS row. Bind off in seed st.

BOTTOM BORDER
Work as for top border, picking up 140 sts along cast-on edge of blanket.

Finishing
Block piece lightly to measurements. ■

Gauge
22 sts and 29 rows to 4"/10cm over St st using size 6 (4mm) circular needle.
Take time to check gauge.

Textured Stripes Hat

Colorful slip-stitch bands give this topper a collegiate feel:
Make it for baby to wear to the big game!

DESIGNED BY LYNN M. WILSON

INTERMEDIATE

Size
Instructions are written for
size 3–6 months.

Knitted measurements
Head circumference
15"/38cm
Depth
6¾"/17cm (excluding earflaps)

Materials
■ 1 3½oz/100g ball (approx 220yd/
201m) of Cascade Yarns *220
Superwash* (superwash wool) each in
#848 blueberry (A), #818 mocha (B)
and #897 baby denim (C)

■ Size 7 (4.5mm) circular needle,
16"/40cm long, *or size to obtain gauge*

■ One set (5) size 7 (4.5mm)
double-pointed needles (dpns)

■ Size G-6 (4mm) crochet hook

■ Stitch holders

■ Stitch marker

Stitch glossary
M1 Insert LH needle from back to front
under the strand between last st worked
and the next st on the LH needle. Knit
into the front loop to twist the st.

Note
When slipping stitches, always hold yarn
on WS of work.

Alternating rib pattern
Rnd 1 K1, [p2, k2] twice, [sl 2 purlwise,
k2] 5 times, [p2, k2] 6 times, [sl 2
purlwise, k2] 5 times, p2, k2, p2, k1.
Rnd 2 K1, [p2, k2] twice, k20, [p2, k2] 6
times, k20, p2, k2, p2, k1.
Rnds 3, 4 and 5 K1, *p2, k2; rep from *,
end p2, k1
Rnds 6 and 7 Sl 1 purlwise, k2, *sl 2
purlwise, k2; rep from *, end sl 1
purlwise.
Rnd 8 Knit.
Rnds 9, 10 and 11 P1, *k2, p2;
rep from *, end k2, p1.
Rnds 12 and 13 K1, *sl 2 purlwise, k2;
rep from *, end sl 2 purlwise, k1.
Rnd 14 Knit.
Rnds 15, 16 and 17 K1, *p2, k2;
rep from *, end k1.
Rep rnds 6–17 for alternating rib pat.

Eaflaps (make 2)
With A, cast on 10 sts.
Row 1 (RS) Sl 1 knitwise, knit to end.
Row 2 Sl 1 knitwise, knit to end.
Row 3 Sl 1 knitwise, k1, M1, p2, k2, p2,
M1, k2—12 sts.
Row 4 Sl 1 knitwise, k1, p1, k2, p2,
k2, p1, k2.
Row 5 Sl 1 knitwise, k1, M1, k1, p2, k2,
p2, k1, M1, k2—14 sts.
Row 6 Sl 1 knitwise, k1, [p2, k2] 3 times.
Cut A. Change to B.
Row 7 Sl 1 knitwise, k1, M1, [sl 2
purlwise, k2] twice, sl 2 purlwise, M1,
k2—16 sts.
Row 8 Sl 1 knitwise, k1, p1, sl 2 purlwise,
[p2, sl 2 purlwise] twice, p1, k2.
Row 9 Sl 1 knitwise, k1, M1, knit to
last 2 sts, M1, k2.—18 sts.
Row 10 Sl 1 knitwise, k1, [p2, k2]
4 times.
Row 11 Sl 1 knitwise, k3, [p2, k2] 3
times, k2.
Row 12 Sl 1 knitwise, k1, [p2, k2] 4
times. Cut B. Change to C.
Row 13 Sl 1 knitwise, k1, [sl 2 purlwise,
k2] 4 times.
Row 14 Sl 1 knitwise, k1, [sl 2 purlwise,
p2] 3 times, sl 2 purlwise, k2.
Row 15 Sl 1 knitwise, knit to end.

Gauge
22 sts and 38 rnds to 4"/10cm over alternating rib pat using size 7 (4.5mm)
circular needle (slightly stretched). *Take time to check gauge.*

Row 16 Sl 1 knitwise, k3, [p2, k2] 3 times, k2.
Row 17 Sl 1 knitwise, k1, [p2, k2] 4 times.
Row 18 Sl 1 knitwise, k1, [k2, p2] 3 times, k4. Place sts on holder.

Hat

With circular needle and A, cast on 9 sts using knitted or cable cast-on method.
With RS facing, work 18 sts from earflap holder as foll: [sl 2 purlwise, k2] 4 times, sl 2 purlwise; cast on 26 sts; rep from * to *; cast on 9 sts—80 sts.
Join and pm for beg of rnds.
Cont in alternating rib pat and stripe sequence as foll:
With A, work rnds 1–5.
With B, work rnds 6–11.
With C, work rnds 12–17.
With A, work rnds 6–11.
With B, work rnds 12–17.
With C, work rnds 6–11.
With A, work rnds 12–17.
With B, work rnds 6–11. Cut B.
With C, work rnds 12–16, ending last rnd 1 st before marker.

CROWN SHAPING

Note Change to dpns (dividing sts evenly between 4 needles) when there are too few sts to work with circular needle.
Rnd (dec) 1 With C, slip last st of rnd onto RH needle, remove marker, slip last st back onto LH needle, replace marker, k2tog (the first and last sts of the rnd), *p2, k2tog; rep from * around—60 sts. Cut C. Change to A.
Rnds 2 and 3 Sl 1 purlwise, *k2, sl 1 purlwise; rep from * around.
Rnd (dec) 4 *K1, k2tog; rep from * around—40 sts.
Rnds 5 and 6 *P1, k1; rep from * around.
Rnd (dec) 7 *K2tog; rep from * around—20 sts. Cut A, leaving an 8"/20.5cm tail, and thread through rem sts. Pull tog tightly and secure end.

Finishing
EDGING

With RS facing and crochet hook, join A with a sl st 2 sts before ear flap join. Ch 1, making sure that work lies flat, sc in 2 cast-on sts, and evenly along outside of ear flap, plus 2 more cast-on sts, closing up any gaps between ear flaps and bottom edge of hat. Fasten off. Work in same way for other ear flap.

TWISTED CORD TIES

For each tie, cut four 12"/30.5cm lengths of each color. Use crochet hook to pull the 12 lengths through the center bottom of an earflap. Even up ends on each side. Holding one end, twist the lengths with the other hand until they double back on themselves. Fold in half, allowing the cord to twist around itself, then tie ends with an overhand knot. Trim ends evenly. Rep for opposite ear flap. ■

Sweet Pea Cardigan

Rows of pods frame the edges of this hooded sweater, while dainty picots give the piece a tender touch.

DESIGNED BY MARY SCOTT HUFF

INTERMEDIATE

Sizes

Instructions are written for size 6 months. Changes for 12 and 18 months are in parentheses.

Knitted measurements

Chest (buttoned) 22 (23½, 25)"/56 (60, 63.5)cm
Length 12 (13, 14)"/30.5 (33, 35.5)cm
Upper arm 10 (11, 12)"/25.5 (28, 30.5)cm

Materials

- 3 (3, 4) 3½oz/100g balls (each approx. 220yd/200m) of Cascade Yarns *220 Superwash* (superwash wool) in #905 celery
- Sizes 4 and 6 (3.5 and 4mm) circular needle, 24"/60cm long *or size to obtain gauge*
- One set (5) szes 4 and 6 (3.5 and 4mm) double-pointed needles (dpns)
- Size E-4 (3.5mm) crochet hook
- 1¼ (1½, 1½)yd/1 (1.4, 1.4)m ³/8"/10mm velvet ribbon (May Arts #PV 34)
- 1¼ (1½, 1½)yd/1 (1.4, 1.4)m ruched ribbon trim (May Arts #360-38-16)
- Three ¾"/19mm buttons (JHB #42068)
- Sewing needle and matching thread
- Cable needle

- Tapestry needle
- Stitch markers
- Stitch holders or waste yarn

Stitch glossary

1 to 4 increase K into (front, back, front, back) of same st.
4 to 1 decrease K3tog tbl, slip this st back to left-hand needle, pass 2nd st over this st.
Make bobble K into (front, back, front) of same st, [sl these 3 sts back to left-hand needle, k3] twice, pass 2nd and 3rd sts over the first st.
Make stem With WS facing, sl 1 st to smaller dpn and cast on 5 sts.
Bind off 6 sts and place rem st back to right-hand needle.
2-st RPC Sl 1 st to cn and hold in *back*, k1, p1 from cn.
2-st LPC Sl 1 st to cn and hold in *front*, p1, k1 from cn.
4-st RKPC Sl 2 sts to cn and hold in *back*, k2, (k1, p1) from cn.
4-st LKPC Sl 2 sts to cn and hold in *front*, (p1, k1), k2 from cn.
3-st RPC Sl 2 sts to cn and hold in *back*, k1, p2 from cn.
3-st LPC Sl 1 st to cn and hold in *front*, p2, k1 from cn.
4-st RPC Sl 1 st to cn and hold in *back*, k3, p1 from cn.
4-st LPC Sl 3 sts to cn and hold in *front*, p1, k3 from cn.
M1R (make 1 right-leaning)
M1L (make 1 left-leaning)

Body

LOWER HEM
With smaller circular needle, cast on 110 (118, 126) sts. Work 6 rows in St st (k on RS, p on WS), beg with a p row.
Turning row (WS) *P2tog, yo; rep to last 2 sts, p2tog—109 (117, 125) sts. Change to larger circular needle and work 6 rows in St st, end with a WS row.
BEG POD PANEL CHARTS
Set-up row (RS) P15 (row 1 of right front pod panel), k79 (87, 95), p15 (row 1 of

Gauge

22 sts and 30 rows to 4"/10cm over St st (k on RS, p on WS) using size 6 (4mm) circular needle. *Take time to check gauge.*

Sweet Pea Cardigan

left front pod panel.
Cont in pats as established, working sts between charts in St st, until body measures 7 (7½, 8)"/18 (19, 20)cm from turning row, end with a WS row.

DIVIDE FOR ARMHOLES
Next row (RS) Work right pod panel and k10 (12, 14) for right front, k4 and place on holder for underarm; k 51 (55, 59) for back, k4 and place on holder for underarm, k10 (12, 14) and work left pod panel for left front.

Left front
Cont in pats on left front sts until front measures 11½ (12½, 13½)"/29 (32, 34)cm from turning row, end with a WS row.

NECK SHAPING
Next row (RS) K10 (12, 14), place pod panel sts on holder.
Work even on rem 10 (12, 14) sts until front measures 12 (13, 14)"/30.5 (33, 35.5)cm from turning row. Place sts on holder.

Right front
With WS facing, attach yarn. Cont in pats on right front sts until front measures 11½ (12½, 13½)"/29 (32, 34)cm from turning row, end with a RS row.

NECK SHAPING
Next row (WS) P10 (12, 14), place pod panel sts on holder.
Work even on rem 10 (12, 14) sts until front measures 12 (13, 14)"/30.5 (33, 35.5)cm from turning row. Place sts on holder.

Back
With WS facing, attach yarn. Work in St st over 51 (55, 59) sts until back measures 12 (13, 14)"/30.5 (33, 35.5)cm from turning row. Place sts on holders as foll: 10 (12, 14) shoulder sts, 31 back neck

sts, 10 (12, 14) shoulder sts. Using 3-needle bind-off, join shoulders.

Hood
With WS facing, place right pod panel sts on larger circular needle. Attach yarn and work next WS row as established. With RS facing, work right pod panel sts, pick up and k4 at right front neck, k 31 back neck sts, pick up and k4 at left front neck, work left pod panel sts—69 sts. P 1 row, marking st at center back neck.
Inc row (RS) Work to 1 st before marked st, M1R, k3, M1L, work to end of row. Rep inc row every RS row 19 times more—109 sts. Work even in pats until hood measures 9 (9½, 10)"/23 (24, 25.5)cm from pick-up row. Join top edge of hood using 3-needle bind-off.

Sleeves
With RS facing and larger dpns, starting at center of underarm, k 2 underarm sts, pick up and k 54 (60, 66) sts around armhole, k 2 underarm sts—58 (64, 70) sts. Pm and join. Knit 5 rnds.
Dec rnd K1, k2tog, k to last 3 sts, ssk, k1. Rep dec rnd every 6th (6th, 5th) rnd 6 (8, 11) times more—44 (46, 46) sts. Change to smaller dpns and k 6 rnds.
Turning rnd *K2tog, yo; rep from *

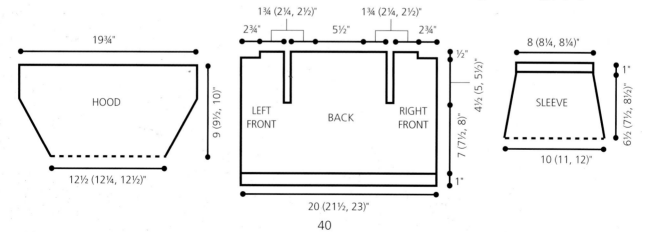

Sweet Pea Cardigan

around. K 6 rnds. Bind off loosely, fold hem to inside and sew invisibly in place.

FRONT EDGE FACING

Fold lower edge hem to inside and sew invisibly in place.

With RS facing and smaller circular needle, starting at lower right front edge, pick up and k210 (226, 240) sts evenly around entire edge, ending at lower left front edge. Work 5 rows in St st.

Turning row (WS) *P2tog, yo; rep from * to last 2 sts, p2tog.

Work 5 rows in St st. Bind off loosely, fold to inside and sew invisibly in place.

Finishing

Block to measurements. Make button loops on right front as foll: with crochet hook, join yarn to edge (between two picots and just below where hood was worked), chain approx 1"/2.5cm, remove hook from loop, skip 2 picots and insert hook into edge then through the loop of chain. Draw yarn through the fabric and through loop on hook. Work a row of sc tightly around the chain. Fasten off. Make tow more loops spaced 2 picots apart. Sew 3 buttons to left front opposite loops. Pin trimmings to fronts and sew invisibly in place.

HOOD TENDRILS (make 3)

With smaller needle, cast on 20 sts.
Row 1 *Kfb; rep from * to end—40 sts.
Using larger needle, bind off loosely.
Sew to point of hood. ■

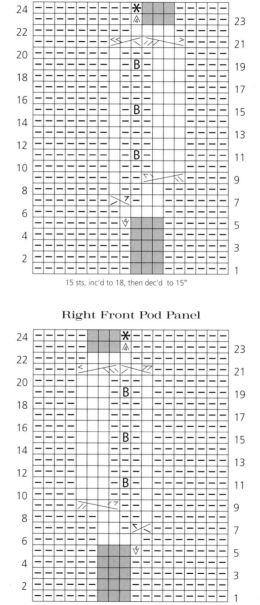

Left Front Pod Panel

15 sts, inc'd to 18, then dec'd to 15"

Right Front Pod Panel

15 sts, inc'd to 18, then dec'd to 15"

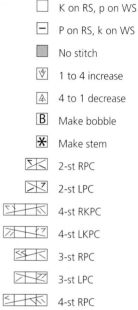

Stitch Key

☐	K on RS, p on WS
⊟	P on RS, k on WS
▨	No stitch
�	1 to 4 increase
⚠	4 to 1 decrease
B	Make bobble
✳	Make stem
	2-st RPC
	2-st LPC
	4-st RKPC
	4-st LKPC
	3-st RPC
	3-st LPC
	4-st RPC
	4-st LPC

Fair Isle Hat and Leg Warmers

Classic color patterning in blue, white and brown creates a set
that is fashion-forward and baby-friendly at the same time.

DESIGNED BY NICHOLE REESE

EXPERIENCED

Size
Instructions are written for
size 6–12 months.

Knitted measurements
HAT
Head circumference 16"/40.5cm
Depth 7¾"/19.5cm
LEG WARMERS
Leg circumference 7"/17.5cm
Length 7"/17.5cm

Materials
■ 1 3½oz/100g ball (approx 220yd/
201m) of Cascade Yarns *220
Superwash* (superwash wool) each
in #1910 summer sky heather (MC),
#1946 silver grey (A) and #1923
red wine heather (B)

HAT
Sizes 4 and 6 (3.5 and 4mm)
circular needles, 16"/40cm length
or size to obtain gauge

■ One set (5) size 6 (4mm)
double-pointed needles (dpns)

■ Stitch marker

LEG WARMERS
■ One set (5) each sizes 5 and 7 (3.75
and 4.5mm) double-pointed needles
(dpns) *or size to obtain gauge*

■ Stitch marker

■ Tapestry needle

Note
To work in the rnd, always read charts
from right to left.

Hat
With smaller circular needle and MC,
cast on 88 sts. Join and pm, taking care
not to twist sts on needles. Work around
in k2, p2 rib for 6 rnds.
Next (inc) rnd K2, p2, M1, [k2,p2] 10
times, M1, [k2,p2] 11 times—90 sts.
Change to larger circular needle. Cont in
St st (knit every rnd) as foll:

BEG CHART PAT I

Rnd 1 Work 9-st rep 10 times. Cont to
foll chart in this way to rnd 19.

BEG CHART PAT II

Rnd 1 Work 2-st rep 45 times. Cont to
foll chart in this way to rnd 5.

BEG CHART III

Rnd 1 Work 9-st rep 10 times. Cont to
foll chart in this way to rnd 9. Do *not*
work rnd 10.
Next (dec) rnd With A, k2tog, k44,
k2tog, knit to end of rnd—88 sts.

CROWN SHAPING
Note Change to dpns (dividing sts evenly
between 4 needles) when there are too
few sts to work with circular needle.
Rnd (dec) 1 With B, *k6, k2tog;
rep from * around—77 sts.

Gauges
HAT 22 sts and 29 rnds to 4"/10cm over St st and chart pats using larger circular needle.
LEG WARMERS 20 sts and 26 rnds to 4"/10cm over St st and chart pats using larger dpns. *Take time to check gauges.*

Fair Isle Hat and Leg Warmers

Rnd 2 With MC, knit.
Rnd (dec) 3 With MC, *k5, k2tog; rep from * around—66 sts.
Rnd 4 With A, knit.
Rnd (dec) 5 With A, *k4, k2tog; rep from * around—55 sts.
Rnd 6 With MC, knit.
Rnd (dec) 7 With MC, *k3, k2tog; rep from * around—44 sts.
Rnd 8 With B, knit. Cut B.
Rnd (dec) 9 With A, *k2, k2tog; rep from * around—33 sts.
Rnd 10 With A, knit. Cut A. Cont with MC only.
Rnd (dec) 11 *K1, k2tog; rep from * around—22 sts.
Rnd 12 Knit.
Rnd (dec) 13 [K2tog] 11 times—11 sts. Cut MC, leaving an 8"/20.5cm tail and thread through rem sts. Pull tog tightly and secure end.

Leg warmers
Beg at ankle, with smaller dpns and MC, loosely cast on 36 sts dividing sts evenly over 4 needles. Join and pm, taking care not to twist sts on needles. Work around in k2, p2 rib for 7 rnds. Change to larger dpns.
Next rnd Knit. Cont in St st as foll:

BEG CHART PAT I
Rnd 1 Work 9-st rep 4 times. Cont to foll chart in this way to rnd 19.

BEG CHART PAT II
Rnd 1 Work 2-st rep 18 times. Cont to foll chart in this way to rnd 5.

BEG CHART III
Rnd 1 Work 9-st rep 4 times. Cont to foll chart in this way to rnd 10.
Next rnd With B, knit. Change to MC and smaller dpns. Work around in k2, p2 rib for 7 rnds. Bind off loosely, or use the sewn bind-off method as foll: Cut MC, leaving a 21"/53.5cm tail. Thread tail in a blunt-tip tapestry needle.

STEP 1
Going from right to left, insert tapestry needle through first 2 sts on LH dpn and pull yarn through.

STEP 2
Going from left to right, insert tapestry needle back through first st and pull yarn through, then drop first st off dpn. Pull on yarn slightly to neaten st. Rep steps 1 and 2 until all sts have been worked off dpn. ■

Chart I
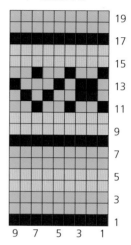

Chart II

Chart III
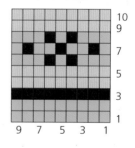

Color Key
Summer Sky Heather (MC)
Silver Grey (A)
Red Wine Heather (B)

<hr />

Patchwork Blanket

Individual squares made up of knits and purls are quick on-the-go projects;
seam them all together for a stunning cover-up!

DESIGNED BY SANDI PROSSER

INTERMEDIATE

Knitted measurements
Approx 32" x 32"/81cm x 81cm

Materials
■ 2 3½oz/100g balls (each approx 220yd/201m) of Cascade Yarns *220 Superwash* (superwash wool) each in #1940 peach (MC), #840 iris (A) and #826 tangerine (B)

■ One pair size 6 (4mm) needles *or size to obtain gauge*

■ Size 6 (4mm) circular needle, 36"/91cm length

Stitch Glossary
M1 Insert LH needle from back to front under the strand between last st worked and the next st on the LH needle. Knit into the front loop to twist the st.

Square I (make 3)
Worked in garter st. With MC, cast on 32 sts. Work in garter st (knit every row) until piece measures 6"/15cm from beg, end with a RS row. Bind off all sts knitwise.

Square II (make 5)
Worked in staggered steps. With MC, cast on 32 sts.
Row 1 and all RS rows Knit.
Rows 2 and 4 *K4, p4; rep from * to end.
Rows 6 and 8 K2, *p4, k4; rep from *, end p4, k2.

Rows 10 and 12 *P4, k4; rep from * to end.
Rows 14 and 16 P2, *k4, p4; rep from *, end k4, p2. Rep rows 1–16 until piece measures 6"/15cm from beg, end with a RS row. Bind off all sts knitwise.

Square III (make 4)
Worked in diagonal blocks. With A, cast on 32 sts.
Row 1 and all RS rows Knit.
Row 2 *K4, p4; rep from * to end.
Row 4 P1, *k4, p4; rep from * , end k4, p3.
Row 6 P2, *k4, p4; rep from *, end k4, p2.
Row 8 P3, *k4, p4; rep from *, end k4, p1.
Row 10 *P4, k4; rep from * to end.
Row 12 *K4, p4; rep from * to end.
Row 14 K3, *p4, k4; rep from *, end p4, k1.
Row 16 K2, *p4, k4; rep from *, end p4, k2.
Row 18 K1, *p4, k4; rep from *, end p4, k3.
Row 20 *P4, k4; rep from * to end. Rep rows 1–20 until piece measures 6"/15cm from beg, end with a RS row. Bind off all sts knitwise.

Gauge
21 sts and 42 rows to 4"/10cm over garter st using size 6 (4mm) needles.
Take time to check gauge.

Patchwork Blanket

Square IV (make 5)

Worked in garter checks. With A, cast on 32 sts.
Rows 1, 3, 5 and 7 (RS) K1, *p5, k5; rep from *, end k1.
Rows 2, 4 and 6 K1, purl to last st, k1.
Rows 8, 10 and 12 K6, *p5, k5; rep from *, end p5, k1.
Rows 9, 11 and 13 Knit.
Row 14 Rep row 12.
Rep rows 1–14 until piece measures 6"/15cm from beg, end with a RS row. Bind off all sts knitwise.

Square V (make 3)

Worked in textured rib. With B, cast on 33 sts.
Rows 1 and 3 (RS) Knit.
Row 2 K2, *p1, k3; rep from *, end p1, k2.
Row 4 P1, *k3, p1; rep from * to end.
Rep rows 1–4 until piece measures 6"/15cm from beg, end with a RS row. Bind off all sts knitwise.

Square VI (make 5)

Worked in chevron st. With B, cast on 32 sts.
Row 1 and all RS rows Knit.
Row 2 K1, *k2, p2, k1, p2, k3; rep from *, end k1.
Row 4 K1, *k1, p2, k3, p2, k2; rep from *, end k1.
Row 6 K1, *p2, k5, p2, k1; rep from *, end k1.
Row 8 K1, *p1, k3, p1, k3, p2; rep from *, end k1.
Row 10 K1, *k3, p3, k3, p1; rep from *, end k1. Rep rows 1–10 until piece measures 6"/15cm from beg, end with a RS row. Bind off all sts knitwise.

Placement Diagram

IV	V	II	III	VI
II	III	VI	I	IV
VI	I	IV	V	II
IV	V	II	III	VI
II	III	VI	I	IV

Finishing

Sew squares together following placement diagram.

MITERED BORDER
With RS facing, circular needle and MC, pick up and k 160 sts evenly spaced across top edge of blanket.
Row 1 (WS) With MC, k1, M1, knit to last st, M1, k1—162 sts.
Row 2 With MC, knit.
Row 3 Rep row 1—164 sts.
Row 4 With A, knit.
Row 5 With A, rep row 1—166 sts.
Row 6 With B, knit.
Row 7 With B, rep row 1—168 sts.
Row 8 With B, knit. Bind off all sts loosely knitwise.
Rep border along 3 rem sides.
Sew mitered edges tog matching stripes.
Block piece lightly to measurements. ■

Flowered Jumper

Delicate border bouquets make this dress ultra-girly,
while the bold color keeps it modern.

DESIGNED BY LOIS YOUNG

Sizes

Instructions are written for size
12 months. Changes for 18 and 24
months are in parentheses.

Knitted measurements

Chest 21 (23, 24)"/53.5 (58.5, 61)cm
Length 16 (17, 19)"/40.5 (43, 48)cm

Materials

- 2 (3, 3) 3½oz/100g balls (each approx
220yd/201m) of Cascade Yarns *220
Superwash* (superwash wool) in #807
raspberry (MC)
- 1 ball each in #851 lime (A) and #914A
tahitian rose (B)
- One pair size 6 (4mm) needles *or size
to obtain gauge*
- Stitch markers
- Two ½"/13mm buttons

Border pattern

(over a multiple of 6 sts plus 1)
Rows 1 and 2 With A, knit.
Rows 3 and 4 With MC, knit.
Rows 5 and 6 With A, knit.
Row 7 (RS) With MC, knit.
Row 8 With MC, purl.
Row 9 With MC, k3, *with A, k1,
with MC, k5; rep from *, end last rep
with MC, k3.
Row 10 With MC, p3, *with A, k1, with
MC, p5; rep from *, end last rep
with MC, p3.
Row 11 With MC, k1, *with A, k5, with
MC, k1; rep from * to end.
Row 12 With MC, p1, *with A, k5, with
MC, p1; rep from * to end.
Rows 13 and 14 Rep rows 9 and 10.
Rows 15 and 16 Rep rows 7 and 8.
Rows 17–22 Rep rows 1–6.
Work rows 1–22 for border pat.

Back

SKIRT
With A, cast on 79 (85, 91) sts. Work
rows 1–22 of border pat. With MC, cont
in St st (knit on RS, purl on WS) until piece
measures 11½ (12, 13½)"/29" (30.5,
34)cm from beg, end with a WS row.
Dec row (RS) K1, *k2tog, k1; rep from *
to end—53 (57, 61) sts. Purl next row.

YOKE
Work rows 1–4 of border pat. With A,
knit next row.

ARMHOLE SHAPING
Next row (WS) With A, bind off first 5
sts knitwise, knit until 43 (47, 51) sts re-
main on RH needle, bind off last 5 sts
knitwise. Turn. Join MC.

Gauges

22 sts and 30 rows to 4"/10cm over St st using size 6 (4mm) needles.
20 sts to 4"/10cm and 22 rows to 2½"/6.5cm over border pat using size 6 (4mm) needles.
20 sts and 48 rows to 4"/10cm over garter st using size 6 (4mm) needles.
Take time to check gauges.

17

Flowered Jumper

Next row (RS) With MC, k 3 (5, 4), pm, k 37 (37, 43), pm, k 3 (5, 4).

Next row With MC, k 3 (5, 4), sl marker, p 37 (37, 43), sl marker, k 3 (5, 4). Keeping 3 (5, 4) sts each side in garter st (knit every row), work rows 9–16 of border pat over center 37 (37, 43) sts, dropping markers on last row. Work pat rows 17–19 of border pat.

NECK SHAPING

Next row (WS) With A, k13, bind off center 17 sts knitwise, knit to end—13 sts each side.

STRAPS

Next row (RS) Join MC, k13; join a 2nd ball of MC, k13. Working both sides at once, work even in garter stitch until armhole measures 4"/10cm, end with a WS row.

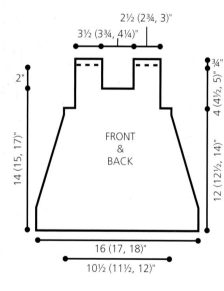

BUTTON BANDS

Cont to work even for 8 rows more. Bind off each side purlwise.

FOR 18 AND 24 MONTHS SIZES ONLY

With MC only, cont in garter st until armhole measures 2½ (3)"/6.5 (7.5)cm, end with a RS row.

NECK SHAPING

Next row (WS) K 14 (15), bind off center 19 (21) sts knitwise, knit to end—14 (15) sts each side.

STRAPS

Working both sides at once, work even in garter stitch until armhole measures 4½ (5)"/11.5 (12.5)cm, end with a WS row.

BUTTON BANDS

Cont to work even for 8 rows more. Bind off each side purlwise.

Front

Work same as back until armhole measures 4 (4½, 5)"/10 (11.5, 12.5)cm, end with a WS row.

BUTTONHOLE BANDS

Cont to work even for 4 rows more.
Next (buttonhole) row (RS) With first ball of MC, k 5 (6, 6), k2tog, yo, k 6 (6, 7); with 2nd ball of MC, k 6 (6, 7), yo, k2tog, k 5 (6, 6). Cont to work even for 3 rows more. Bind off each side purlwise.

Finishing

Block pieces to measurements. To embellish the center of each flower, use B to embroider 3 vertical satin stitches over center sts of rows 11 and 12. Sew side seams. Sew on buttons. ■

18

Songbird Sweater

A sweet chickadee, knit in intarsia, sings on the front of this pullover,
while a row of flowers borders the hem.

DESIGNED BY PAT OLSKI

INTERMEDIATE

Sizes

Instructions are written for size 6 months. Changes for 12 and 18 months are in parentheses.

Knitted measurements

Chest 19 (21, 23)"/48 (53.5, 58.5)cm
Length 12 (12½, 13)"/30.5 (32, 33)cm
Upper arm 8 (9, 10)"/20.5 (23, 25.5)cm

Materials

- 2 (2, 3) 3½oz/100g balls (each approx 220yd/201m) of Cascade Yarns *220 Superwash* (superwash wool) in #1914 alaska sky (MC)
- 1 ball each in #818 mocha (A), #1921 persimmon (B), #846 blue (C) and #839 medium rose (D)
- One pair each sizes 4 and 6 (3.5 and 4mm) needles *or size to obtain gauge*
- Stitch holder
- Three ⅝"/16mm buttons

Stitch glossary

MB (make bobble) [K1, p1] twice in same st, making 4 sts from one; then pass the 3rd, 2nd and first sts over the last st made.
M1 Insert LH needle from back to front under the strand between last st worked and the next st on the LH needle. Knit into the front loop to twist the st.

K1, p1 rib

(multiple of 2 sts plus 1)
Row 1 (RS) K1, *p1, k1; rep from * to end.
Row 2 P1, *k1, p1; rep from * to end.
Rep rows 1 and 2 for k1, p1 rib.

Back

With smaller needles and A, cast on 53 (59, 65) sts. Work in k1, p1 rib for 1½"/4cm, end with a WS row. Change to larger needles and St st (k on RS, p on WS). Work first stripe pat as foll: 3 rows B, 2 rows MC and 1 row C.
Cont in pat st as foll:
Row 1 (RS) K 2 (5, 8) with B, [p7 with D, k7 with B] 3 times, p7 with D, k 2 (5, 8) with B.
Row 2 P 2 (5, 8) with B, [k7 with D, p7 with B] 3 times, k7 with D, p 2 (5, 8) with B.
Row 3 K 2 (5, 8) with B, [p3 with D, MB with B, p3 with D, k7 with B] 3 times, p3 with D, MB with B, p3 with D, k 2 (5, 8) with B.
Row 4 Rep row 2.
Row 5 Rep row 1.
Row 6 Rep row 2. Work second stripe pat as foll: 2 rows MC and 2 rows A.
Cont with MC only. Work even until piece measures 11½ (12, 12½)"/29 (30.5,32)cm from beg, end with a WS row.

NECK AND SHOULDER SHAPING

Next row (RS) K 17 (19, 22), join another ball of MC and bind off center 19 (21, 21) sts, knit to end. Working both sides at once, dec 1 st from each neck edge once. Work even on 16 (18, 21) sts each side until piece measures 12 (12½, 13)"/30.5 (32, 33)cm from beg, end with a WS row. Bind off first 16 (18, 21) sts for right shoulder, work rem 16 (18, 21) sts as foll:

BUTTON BAND

Change to smaller needles. Work in k1, p1 rib for 5 rows. Bind off in rib.

Front

Work same as back until second stripe pat is completed, end with a WS row.

BEG CHART PAT

Row 1 (RS) K 14 (17, 20), work 19 sts of chart, k 20 (23, 26). Cont to foll chart in this way to row 24, then work with MC only. Work even until piece measures 10 (10½, 11)"/25.5 (26.5, 28)cm from beg, end with a WS row.

NECK SHAPING

Next row (RS) K 20 (22, 25), join another ball of MC and bind off center 13 (15, 15) sts, knit to end. Working both sides at once, work next row even. Dec 1 st

Gauge

22 sts and 30 rows to 4"/10cm over St st using larger needles. *Take time to check gauge.*

Songbird Sweater

from each neck edge on next row, then every other row 3 times more. Work even on 16 (18, 21) sts each side until piece measures 11½ (12, 12½)"/29 (30.5, 31.5)cm from beg, end with a WS row.

SHOULDER SHAPING
Next row (RS) Place first 16 (18, 21) sts on holder for left shoulder/buttonhole band. Cont to work on rem 16 (18, 21) sts for right shoulder until piece measures same length as back to shoulder, end with a WS row. Bind off.

BUTTONHOLE BAND
Place sts from holder onto smaller needle ready for a RS row. Work in k1, p1 rib for 2 rows.
Next (buttonhole) row (RS) Work in rib over first 3 (4, 5) sts, k2tog, yo, work in rib over next 5 (6, 7) sts, yo, k2tog, work in rib over last 4 (4, 5) sts. Cont in rib for 2 rows more. Bind off in rib.

Sleeves
With smaller needles and A, cast on 37 (39, 41) sts. Work in k1 p1 rib for 1½"/4cm, end with a WS row. Change to larger needles and St st. Work in stripe pat as foll: 3 rows B, 2 rows MC, 1 row C and 2 rows D. Cont with MC only.
Inc row (RS) K2, M1, knit to last 2 sts, M1, k2. Rep inc row every 12th (8th, 8th) row 3 (5, 7) times more—45 (51, 57) sts. Work even until piece measures 8½ (9, 10)"/21.5 (23, 25.5)cm from beg, end with a WS row. Bind off.

Finishing
Lightly block pieces to measurements.

EMBROIDERY
Referring to chart, embroider a French knot eye using A, and straight stitch legs,

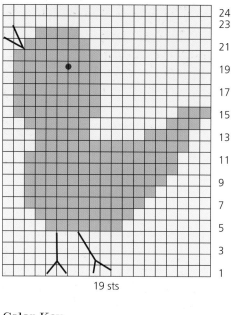

19 sts

Color Key

☐ Alaska Sky (MC)

▨ Blue (C)

Stitch Key

| Straight stitch using Persimmon (B)

● French Knot using Mocha (A)

feet and beak using B. Referring to photo, use A to embroider a chain stitch branch. Using A, embroider a long lazy daisy stitch leaf on each side of each bobble flower. Sew right shoulder seam.

NECKBAND
With RS facing, smaller needles and MC, pick up and k 4 sts along side edge of buttonhole band, 34 (36, 36) sts along front neck edge to right shoulder, 24 (26,

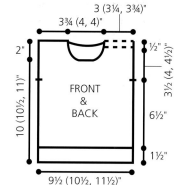

26) sts along back neck edge, then 4 sts along side edge of button band—66 (70 (70) sts. Work in k1, p1 rib for 2 rows.
Next (buttonhole) row (WS) Work in rib to last 5 sts, k2tog, yo, k3. Cont to work in rib for 2 rows. Bind off in rib. Sew on buttons. Button shoulder closed. Place markers 4 (4½, 5)"/10 (11.5, 12.5)cm down from shoulders on back and front. Sew sleeves to armholes between markers. Sew side and sleeve seams. ▨

SLEEVE

8 (9, 10)"

7 (7½, 8½)"

1½"

6 (6½, 6¾)"

3 (3¼, 3¾)"
3¾ (4, 4)"

2"

½"

FRONT & BACK

10 (10½, 11)"

3½ (4, 4½)"

6½"

1½"

9½ (10½, 11½)"

Faux Entrelac Blanket

An unusual shape and alternating squares of stockinette stitch and garter stitch create a cozy throw that looks more difficult to knit than it is.

DESIGNED BY CANDACE EISNER STRICK

INTERMEDIATE

Knitted measurements
Approx 37½" x 42½"/95cm x 108cm

Materials
■ 2 3½oz/100g balls (each approx 220yd/201m) of Cascade Yarns *220 Superwash* (superwash wool) each in #840 iris (A) and #894 strawberry cream (B)

■ Size 7 (4.5mm) circular needle, 36"/91cm length *or size to obtain gauge*

■ Spare size 7 (4.5mm) needle for casting on sts

Note
Use the long-tail method of casting on throughout.

Blanket
FIRST COURSE
With circular needle and A, cast on 25 sts.
Row 1 Sl 1 purlwise wyif, knit to end. Rep this row 47 times more—24 garter st ridges. Cut yarn.

SECOND COURSE
With spare needle and B, cast on 25 sts. Cut yarn. With RS of first course facing, place cast-on sts onto LH end of circular needle so that yarn tails are at your right. With RH end of circular needle and B, cast on 25 sts—75 sts on circular needle.
Row 1 (RS) Sl 1 purlwise wyif, knit to end.
Row 2 Sl 1 purlwise wyif, k24, p25, k25. Rep rows 1 and 2 twenty-three times more. Cut yarn.

THIRD COURSE
With spare needle and A, cast on 25 sts. Cut yarn. With RS of second course facing, place cast-on sts onto LH end of circular needle so that yarn tails are at your right. With RH end of circular needle and A, cast on 25 sts—125 sts on circular needle.
Row 1 (RS) Sl 1 purlwise wyif, knit to end.
Row 2 Sl 1 purlwise wyif, k24, [p25, k25] twice. Rep rows 1 and 2 twenty-three times more. Cut yarn.

Gauges
19 sts and 38 rows to 4"/10cm over garter st (k every row) using size 7 (4.5mm) circular needle.
21 sts and 26 rows to 4"/10cm over St st (k on RS, p on WS) using size 7 (4.5mm) circular needle. *Take time to check gauges.*

Faux Entrelac Blanket

FOURTH COURSE

With spare needle and B, cast on 25 sts. Cut yarn. With RS of third course facing, place cast-on sts onto LH end of circular needle so that yarn tails are at your right. With RH end of circular needle and B, cast on 25 sts—175 sts on circular needle.

Row 1 (RS) Sl 1 purlwise wyif, knit to end.

Row 2 Sl 1 purlwise wyif, k24, [p25, k25] 3 times. Rep rows 1 and 2 twenty-two times more, then row 1 once.

Next row (WS) Bind off first 25 sts, work to end—150 sts.

Next row (RS) Bind off first 25 sts—125 sts rem on needle. Cut yarn.

FIFTH COURSE

With A, work as foll:

Row 1 (RS) Sl 1 purlwise wyif, knit to end.

Row 2 Sl 1 purlwise wyif, k24, [p25, k25] twice. Rep rows 1 and 2 twenty-two times more, then row 1 once.

Next row (WS) Bind off first 25 sts, work to end—100 sts.

Next row (RS) Bind off first 25 sts—75 sts rem on needle. Cut yarn.

SIXTH COURSE

With B, work as foll:

Row 1 (RS) Sl 1 purlwise wyif, knit to end.

Row 2 Sl 1 purlwise wyif, k24, p25, k25. Rep rows 1 and 2 twenty-two times more, then row 1 once.

Next row (WS) Bind off first 25 sts, work to end—50 sts.

Next row (RS) Bind off first 25 sts—25 sts rem on needle. Cut yarn.

SEVENTH COURSE

With A, work as foll:

Row 1 Sl 1 purlwise wyif, knit to end. Rep this row 46 times more, ending with a RS row. Bind off all sts knitwise.

Finishing

Block piece lightly to measurements. ■

Quick Tip

If you prefer a more graphic look, swap the soft, monochromatic colors for complementary hues.

Striped Socks

Change the colors of these simple footies to customize them for every baby on your gift list.

DESIGNED BY VERONICA MANNO

INTERMEDIATE

Size
Instructions are written for size 6 months.

Knitted measurements
Foot circumference 5½"/14cm
Foot length 4"/10cm

Materials
■ 1 3½oz/100g ball (approx 220yd/200m) of Cascade Yarns *220 Superwash* (superwash wool) each in #910A winter white (A) and #812 turquoise (B)

■ One set (5) size 5 (3.75mm) double-pointed needles (dpns) *or size to obtain gauge*

■ Stitch marker

Note
When working stripes, carry color not in use up WS of work.

Sock (make 2)
CUFF
With dpn and A, cast on 28 sts. Divide sts over 4 needles (7 sts on each). Join, taking care not to twist sts on needles, pm for beg of rnds. Work in k2, p2 rib for 4 rnds. Cont in St st (knit every rnd) and stripe pat as foll: 3 rnds B, 4 rnds A, 4 rnds B and 4 rnds A. Cont with A as foll:

BEG HEEL FLAP
Note Heel flap is worked back and forth on one needle over half the sts; 14 rem sts are on hold.
Next row (RS) With free needle, k7 sts from first needle; turn.
Next row P 7 sts from first needle, then p7 sts from 4th needle; turn—14 sts.
Row 1 (RS) [Sl 1, k1] 7 times.
Row 2 Sl 1, p13. Rep rows 1 and 2 five times more, then row 1 once.

TURN HEEL
Row 1 (WS) P9, p2tog, p1; turn.
Row 2 Sl 1, k5, k2tog, k1; turn.
Row 3 Sl 1, purl to 1 st before last turn (gap created by turn in previous row), p2tog, p1; turn.
Row 4 Sl 1, knit to 1 st before last turn, k2tog, k1—10 heel sts.

GUSSET
Next rnd With free needle and working yarn, pick up and k 8 sts along side edge of heel flap, with free needle k 7 sts from Needle 2, with free needle k 7 sts from Needle 3, with free needle, pick up and k 8 sts along opposite side edge of heel flap, with same needle k first 5 sts of heel—40 sts. Distribute sts so there are 13 sts each on Needle 1 and Needle 4, and 7 sts each on Needles 2 and 3. Working yarn is located at center of heel. Pm for beg of rnds.
Next rnd Knit. Change to B.
Dec rnd *Needle 1* k to last 3 sts, k2tog, k1; *Needles 2 and 3* knit; *Needle 4* k1, ssk, knit to end—38 sts. Rep dec rnd twice more—34 sts. Change to A. Rep dec rnd three times more—28 sts (7 sts on each needle). Cont with A as foll:

FOOT
Knit next 2 rnds. Change to B and knit next 3 rnds. Change to A and knit next 5 rnds. Change to B and cont as foll:

TOE
Dec rnd *Needle 1* k to last 3 sts, k2tog, k1; *Needle 2* k1, ssk, knit to end; *Needle 3* knit to last 3 sts, k2tog, k1; *Needle 4* k1, ssk, knit to end—24 sts. Rep dec rnd 4 times more—8 sts.
Cut yarn, leaving a 6"/15cm tail and thread through rem sts. Pull tog tightly and secure end. ■

Gauge
20 sts and 28 rnds to 4"/10cm over St st using size 5 (3.75mm) dpns.
Take time to check gauge.

Raglan Cardigan

Raglan shaping and simple garter stitch borders are all this
sweater needs to make it special.

DESIGNED BY THERESE CHYNOWETH

INTERMEDIATE

Sizes
Instructions are written for size 6 months.
Changes for 12 and 18 months are in
parentheses.

Finished measurements
Chest (closed)
22 (24, 26)"/56 (61, 66)cm
Length
11½ (12½, 13½)"/29 (31.5, 34)cm
Upper arm
7½ (8½, 9½)"/19 (21.5, 24)cm

Materials
■ 2 (3, 3) 3½oz/100g balls (each approx
220yd/201m) of Cascade Yarns *220
Superwash Quatro* (superwash wool) in
#1928 oceanside

■ Size 7 (4.5mm) circular needle,
24"/61cm length *or size to obtain gauge*

■ One pair size 7 (4.5mm) needles

■ Stitch holders

■ Stitch markers

■ One ¾"/19mm button

Note
Body is worked in one piece to the
underarms.

Stitch glossary
kf&b Inc 1 by knitting into the front and
back of the next st.

Sleeves
With straight needles, cast on 23 (25, 27)
sts. Work in garter st (knit every row)
for 8 rows. Cont in St st (knit on RS, purl
on WS) and work even for 2 rows.
Inc row (RS) K1, kf&b, knit to last 2 sts,
kf&b, k1. Rep inc row every 4th row 3 (6,
7) times more, then every 6th row 2 (0,
0) times—35 (39, 43) sts. Work even until
piece measures 6 (6½, 7½)"/15 (16.5,
19)cm from beg, end with a WS row.
Bind off 4 sts at beg of next 2 rows. Place
rem 27 (31, 35) sts on holder.
Set aside.

Body
With circular needle, cast on 113 (121,
129) sts. Work in garter st for 8 rows.
Next row (RS) K5 (right front band), pm,
k to last 5 sts, pm, k5 (left front band).
Next row K5, sl marker, purl to next
marker, sl marker, k5. Keeping 5 sts each
side in garter st for front bands, work
rem sts in St st. Work even until piece
measures 8 (8½, 9)"/20.5 (21.5, 23)cm
from beg, end with a RS row.

DIVIDE FOR FRONTS AND BACK
Next row (WS) K5, drop marker, p 21
(23, 25) sts, bind off next 6 sts for left
underarm, p until there are 49 (53, 57)
sts on RH needle after bind-off, bind off
next 6 sts for right underarm, p until
there are 21 (23, 25) sts on RH needle
after 2nd bind-off, drop marker, k5.

Yoke
Next row (RS) K 26 (28, 30) for right
front, pm, k 27 (31, 35) sts from sleeve
holder, pm, k 49 (53, 57) sts for back,
pm, k 27 (31, 35) sts from 2nd sleeve
holder, pm, k 26 (28, 30) sts for left
front—155 (171, 187) sts.
Next row (WS) K5, *p to 2 sts before
marker, k2, sl marker, k2; rep from * 3
times more, purl to last 5 sts, k5.
Note Read through entire dec and neck
shaping directions before you beg.
Dec row 1 (RS) *Knit to 3 sts before
marker, k2tog, k1, sl marker, k1, ssk; rep
from * 3 more times, knit to end—
147(163, 179) sts.
Next row K5, *purl to 2 sts before next
marker, k2, sl marker, k2; rep from *
3 more times, purl to last 5 sts, k5. Rep
last 2 rows 4 (6, 8) more times—115 sts.
Decrease only on fronts, fronts of sleeves,
and back as foll:

Gauge
19 sts and 26 rows to 4"/10cm over St st using size 7 (4.5mm) circular needle.
Take time to check gauge.

Raglan Cardigan

Dec row 2 (RS) Knit to 3 sts before marker, k2tog, k1, sl marker, k1, ssk, knit to and sl next marker, k1, ssk, knit to 3 sts before next marker, k2tog, k1, sl marker, knit to 3 sts before next marker, k2tog, k1, sl marker, k1, ssk, knit to end—109 sts. Work 1 row even.

Next row (RS) Rep Dec row 1 once more - 101 sts. Work 1 row even.

Rep last 4 rows once more—87 sts. Decrease only on back and shape neck as foll:

Dec row 3 (RS) Knit to second marker, sl marker, k1, ssk, k to 3 sts before next marker, k2tog, k1, sl marker, knit to end—85 sts. Work 1 row even. Rep last 2 rows 4 times more, AT THE SAME TIME, when piece measures approx 10 (11, 12)/25.5 (28, 30.5)cm from beg, bind off from each neck edge 7 sts once, 5 sts once, 4 sts once, 3 sts once, 2 sts twice,

then 1 st once, end with a WS row—29 sts. The 2 back markers are still in place, cut yarn and leave sts on needle.

Neckband
With RS facing and straight needles, pick up and k 25 along right front neck and top of right sleeve; work sts from needle as foll: k1, k2tog, k1, drop marker, k1, ssk, knit to 3 sts before next marker, k2tog, k1, drop marker, k1, ssk, k1; pick up and k 25 sts along top of left sleeve and left front neck—75 sts.
Next (buttonhole) row (WS) Knit to last 5 sts, bind off next 2 sts, knit to end.
Next (dec) row (RS) K3, cast on 2 sts over bound-off sts, knit to end and dec 4 sts evenly spaced across—71 sts.
Knit next 4 rows. Bind off knitwise.

Finishing
Sew sleeve seams. Sew bound-off edges of sleeves to bound-off edges of armholes. Block piece to measurements. Sew on button. ▪

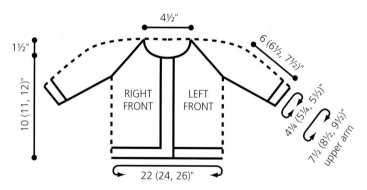

Colorblock Beret

Graphic stripes in subtle shades of gray, black, white and lavender form a spiral effect in this snazzy topper.

DESIGNED BY ANASTASIA BLAES

Size
Instructions are written for size 6–12 months.

Knitted measurements
Head circumference 16"/40.5cm

Materials
■ 1 3½oz/100g ball (approx 220yd/201m) of Cascade Yarns *220 Superwash* (superwash wool) each in #815 black (A), #1944 westpoint blue heather (B), #900 charcoal (C) and #1946 silver grey (D)

■ One pair size 6 (4mm) needles *or size to obtain gauge*
■ One set (5) size 6 (4mm) double-pointed needles (dpns)
■ Stitch marker

Stitch glossary
s2pp2 Slip 2 stitches together purlwise, purl 1, pass the 2 slip stitches over the purl 1.

Hat crown
FIRST TRIANGLE
With straight needles and A, cast on 25 sts.

Row 1 (WS) Sl first st purlwise (selvage), knit to end. Change to B.
Row 2 Sl first st purlwise, knit to end.
Row 3 Sl first st purlwise, purl to last st, k1.
Row 4 Sl first st purlwise, knit to end.
Row (dec) 5 Sl first st purlwise, p2tog, purl to last 3 sts, p2tog tbl, k1—23 sts.
Row 6 Sl first st purlwise, knit to end.
Row 7 Sl first st purlwise, purl to last st, k1. Change to A.
Row 8 Sl first st purlwise, knit to end.
Row (dec) 9 Sl first st purlwise, k2tog, knit to last 3 sts, ssk, k1—21 sts. Change to C.
Rows 10–15 With C, rep rows 2–7—19 sts. Change to A.
Row 16 Sl first st purlwise, knit to end.
Row (dec) 17 Sl first st purlwise, k2tog, knit to last 3 sts, ssk, k1—17 sts. Change to D.
Rows 18–23 With D, rep rows 2–7—15 sts. Change to A.
Row 24 Sl first st purlwise, knit to end.
Row (dec) 25 Sl first st purlwise, k2tog, knit to last 3 sts, ssk, k1—13 sts. Change to B.
Rows 26–44 Rep rows 2–20, changing colors as stated—5 sts.

Gauge
23 sts and 34 rows to 4"/10cm over St (knit on RS, purl on WS) st using size 6 (4mm) needles.
Take time to check gauge.

Colorblock Beret

Row (dec) 45 Sl first st purlwise, s2pp2, k1—3 sts.
Row 46 Sl first st purlwise, k2.
Row (dec) 47 S2pp2—1 st. Fasten off.

SECOND TRIANGLE
Position first triangle so RS is facing and cast-on edge is at your right. With straight needles and A, pick up and k 25 sts evenly spaced along selvage edge. Work rows 1–47 as for first triangle.

THIRD TRIANGLE
Position second triangle so RS is facing and pick-up row is at your right. With straight needles and A, pick up and k 25 sts evenly spaced along selvage edge. Work rows 1–47 as for first triangle.

FOURTH AND FIFTH TRIANGLES
Rep as for third triangle twice more—5 connected triangles. Using A, sew cast-on edge of first triangle to selvage edge of fifth triangle. Lightly block to a 9"/23cm diameter circle.

BRIM
With RS facing, dpn and A, beg at point of first triangle and pick up and k 125 sts evenly spaced around selvage edge of crown. Divide sts evenly over 4 needles. Join and pm for beg of rnds. Purl 1 rnd, knit 1 rnd, purl 1 rnd. Change to B. Knit next rnd.

Dec rnd 1 *K23, k2tog; rep from * around—120 sts. Knit next rnd.
Dec rnd 2 *K22, k2tog; rep from * around—115 sts. Knit next rnd.
Dec rnd 3 *K21, k2tog; rep from * around—110 sts. Knit next rnd.
Dec rnd 4 *K20, k2tog; rep from * around—105 sts. Knit next rnd.
Dec rnd 5 *K19, k2tog; rep from * around—100 sts. Knit next rnd.
Dec rnd 6 *K18, k2tog; rep from * around—95 sts. Knit next rnd.
Dec rnd 7 *K17, k2tog; rep from * around—90 sts. Knit next rnd.
Dec rnd 8 *K16, k2tog; rep from * around—85 sts. Knit next rnd.
Dec rnd 9 *K15, k2tog; rep from * around—80 sts. Cut B. Change to A. Knit next rnd. Work in k1, p1 rib for ¾"/2cm. Bind off loosely in rib. ■

Quick Tip
The construction of this sweet beret is a little unusual. It's a good idea—as always—to read through the pattern completely before beginning to knit.

Purple Poppies Cardigan

Large contrasting flowers dot the body of this grassy green jacket.
Ring in spring and ward off winter's last chill!

DESIGNED BY HEIDI KOZAR

EXPERIENCED

Sizes

Instructions are written for size 6 months. Changes for 12 and 18 months are in parentheses.

Knitted measurements

Chest (closed) 21 (23, 25)"/53.5 (58.5, 63.5)cm
Length 12½ (13½, 14½)"/31.5 (34, 37)cm
Upper arm 8 (9, 10)"/20.5 (23, 25.5)cm

Materials

■ 2 (2, 3) 3½oz/100g balls (each approx 220yd/201m) of Cascade Yarns *220 Superwash Quatro* (superwash wool) in #1930 green tea (MC)

■ 1 (1, 2) 3½oz/100g balls (each approx 220yd/201m) of Cascade Yarns *220 Superwash* (superwash wool) each in #842 light iris (A)

■ 1 ball in #820 lemon (B)

■ Size 6 (4mm) circular needle, 32"/81cm length *or size to obtain gauge*

■ One pair size 6 (4mm) needles

■ Stitch holders

■ Five ⁹⁄₁₆"/14mm buttons

Note

Body is worked in one piece to the underarms.

K1, p1 rib

(over a multiple of 2 sts plus 1)
Row 1 (WS) P1, *k1, p1; rep from * to end.
Row 2 K1, *p1, k1; rep from * to end.
Rep rows 1 and 2 for k1, p1 rib.

Body

With circular needle and A, cast on 105 (115, 125) sts. Work in St st (k on RS, p on WS) for 7 rows. Knit next WS row for turning ridge. Beg with a k row, cont in St st for 2 rows.

BEG CHART PAT

Row 1 (RS) Beg with st 11 (6, 1) and work to st 37, work 26-st rep 3 times more, then work to st 37 (42, 47).
Row 2 Beg with st 37 (42, 47) and work to st 12, work 26-st rep 3 times more, then work to st 11 (6, 1). Cont to foll chart in this way to row 36, then rep rows 1–36 to end. Work even until piece measures 8½ (9, 9½)"/21.5 (23, 24)cm

above turning ridge, end with a WS row.
DIVIDE FOR FRONTS AND BACK

Next row (RS) K 22 (25, 27) sts, place these sts on holder for right front, bind off next 4 sts for right underarm, knit until there are 53 (57, 63) sts on RH needle, leave these sts on needle for back, bind off next 4 sts for left underarm, knit to end, place these last 22 (25, 27) sts on holder for left front.

BACK

Change to straight needles. Cont to foll chart pat as established until armhole measures 4 (4½, 5)"/10 (11.5, 12.5)cm, end with a WS row. Bind off all sts.

LEFT FRONT

Place 22 (25, 27) sts from left front holder onto straight needles ready for a WS row. Cont to foll chart pat as established until armhole measures 2½ (3, 3½)"/6.5 (7.5, 9)cm, end with a RS row.

Gauge

26 sts to 5"/12.5cm and 24 rows to 4"/10cm over St st and chart pat using size 6 (4mm) circular needle.
Take time to check gauge.

Purple Poppies Cardigan

NECK SHAPING
Bind off 6 (7, 7) sts at beg of next row.
Next (dec) row (RS) Knit to last 3 sts, k2tog, k1. Work next row even. Rep last 2 rows 3 times more—12 (14, 16) sts. Work even until piece measures same length as back to shoulder, end with a WS row. Bind off.

RIGHT FRONT
Place 22 (25, 27) sts from right front holder onto straight needles ready for a WS row. Cont to foll chart pat as established until armhole measures 2½ (3, 3½)"/6.5 (7.5, 9)cm, end with a WS row.

NECK SHAPING
Bind off 6 (7, 7) sts at beg of next row. Work next row even.
Next (dec) row (RS) K1, ssk, knit to end. Work next row even. Rep last 2 rows 3 times more—12 (14, 16) sts. Work even until piece measures same length as back to shoulder, end with a WS row. Bind off.

Sleeves
With straight needles and B, cast on 32 (34, 36) sts. Work in St st for 6 rows. Change to A. Knit next 2 rows (for turning ridge). Beg with a k row, cont in St st for 2 rows.

BEG CHART PAT
Row 1 (RS) With MC, k 3 (4, 5), work 26-st rep once, with MC, k 3 (4, 5).
Row 2 With MC, p 3 (4, 5), work 26-st

rep once, with MC, p 3 (4, 5). Cont to foll chart in this way to row 18, then work with MC only. AT THE SAME TIME, when piece measures 1"/2.5 above turning ridge, inc 1 st each side on next row, then every 4th row 0 (2, 5) times more, then every 6th row 4 (4, 3) times—42 (48, 54) sts. Work even until piece measures 6 (6½, 7½)" above turning ridge, end with a WS row. Bind off.

Finishing
Block pieces to measurements. Referring to chart, embroider French knots in center of each flower using B. Sew shoulder seams. Turn hem of body to WS along turning ridge and sew in place.

BUTTON BAND
With RS facing, straight needles and MC, pick up and k 55 (59, 63) sts evenly spaced along left front edge. Work in k1,

p1 rib for 5 rows. Change to A. Knit next row. Cont in k1, p1 rib for 1 row more. Bind off in rib. Place markers for 4 buttonholes on right front edge, with the first ¾"/2cm from lower edge, the last 2½"/4cm from neck edge and 2 more evenly spaced between.

BUTTONHOLE BAND
With RS facing, straight needles and MC, pick up and k 55 (59, 63) sts evenly spaced along right front edge. Work in k1, p1 rib for 3 rows.
Next (buttonhole) row (RS) *Work in rib to marker, k2tog, yo; rep from * 3 times more, work in rib to end. Work in rib for 1 row more. Change to A. Knit next row. Cont in k1, p1 rib for 1 row more. Bind off in rib.

NECKBAND
With RS facing, straight needles and MC, pick up and k 22 (23, 23) sts spaced along right neck edge to shoulder seam, 29 (29, 31) sts along back neck edge to next shoulder seam, then 22 (23, 23) sts along left neck edge. Work in k1, p1 rib for 3 rows.
Next (buttonhole) row (RS) K1, p1, k2tog, yo, work in rib to end. Work in rib for 1 row more. Change to A. Knit next row. Cont in k1, p1 rib for 1 row more. Bind off in rib. Sew sleeve seams. Turn hem of each sleeve to WS along turning ridge and sew in place. Set in sleeves. Sew on buttons. ■

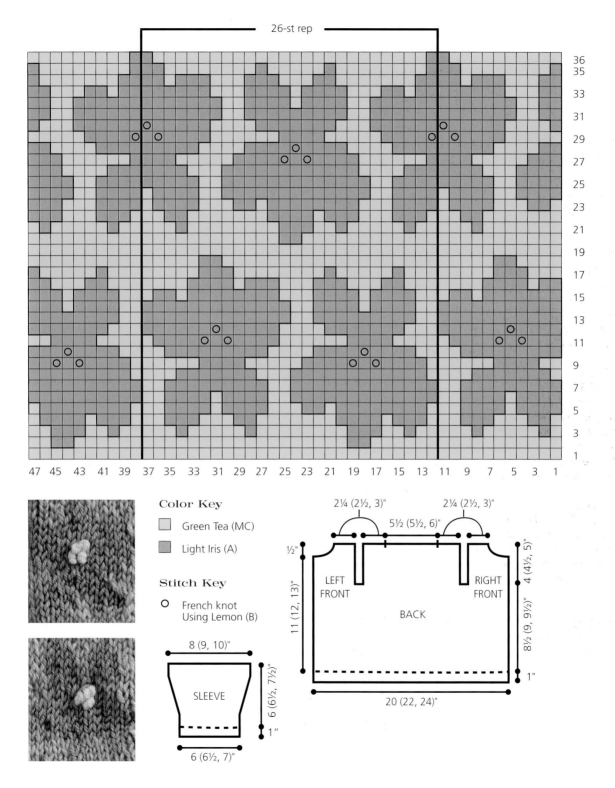

26-st rep

Color Key

- ☐ Green Tea (MC)
- ▨ Light Iris (A)

Stitch Key

- ○ French knot
  Using Lemon (B)

8 (9, 10)"

SLEEVE

6 (6½, 7½)"

1"

6 (6½, 7)"

2¼ (2½, 3)" 5½ (5½, 6)" 2¼ (2½, 3)"

½"

LEFT FRONT

RIGHT FRONT

BACK

11 (12, 13)"

4 (4½, 5)"

8½ (9, 9½)"

1"

20 (22, 24)"

Striped Leg Warmers

Baby fussy about wearing socks or booties? Keep tiny legs warm with these fun warmers that can't be kicked off.

DESIGNED BY CHERYL MURRAY

INTERMEDIATE

Size

Instructions are written for size 6–12 months.

Knitted measurements

Leg circumference 7"/17.5cm
Length 10"/25.5cm

Materials

- 1 3½oz/100g ball (approx 220yd/201m) of Cascade Yarns *220 Superwash* (superwash wool) each in #826 tangerine (MC) and #905 celery (CC)
- One set (5) each sizes 5 and 7 (3.75 and 4.5mm) double-pointed needles (dpns) or size to obtain gauge
- Stitch marker

Stripe pattern

Working in St st, *work 6 rnds MC, 2 rnds CC, 2 rnds MC, 2 rnds CC; rep from * (12 rnds) for stripe pat.

Leg warmers

Beg at ankle ruffle, with larger dpns and CC, cast on 96 sts, dividing sts evenly over 4 needles. Join and pm, taking care not to twist sts on needles. Work around in garter st (knit 1 rnd, purl 1 rnd) for 8 rnds.
Dec rnd *K3tog; rep from * around—32 sts. Change to smaller dpns and work around in k2, p2 rib for 9 rnds. Change to larger dpns. Cont in St st (knit *every* rnd) and stripe pat. AT THE SAME TIME, beg to shape leg on first rnd as foll:
Inc rnd 1 With MC, k1, M1, knit to end—33 sts. Work even until first stripe rep (12 rnds) has been completed.
Inc rnd 2 With MC, knit to last st, M1, k1—34 sts. Work even until second stripe rep (24 rnds) has been completed.
Inc rnd 3 Rep inc rnd 1—35 sts. Work even until third stripe rep (36 rnds) has been completed.
Inc rnd 4 Rep inc rnd 2—36 sts. Work even in stripe pat until piece measures 8½"/21.5cm from beg. Cut MC. Cont with CC only. Change to smaller dpns and work around in k2, p2 rib for 1½"/4cm. Bind off loosely in rib. ■

Gauge

20 sts and 28 rnds to 4"/10cm over St st using larger dpns.
Take time to check gauge.

Sheep Pillow

There's no need to count sheep when your toddler has this comfy cushion to nap with. It's as much a toy as it is décor.

DESIGNED BY AMY BAHRT

■■■□
INTERMEDIATE

Knitted measurements
Approx 19¾" x 18½"/50cm x 47cm (excluding tail)

Materials
■ 1 3½oz/100g ball (approx 220yd/ 201m) of Cascade Yarns *220 Superwash* (superwash wool) each in #1926 doeskin heather (A), #862 walnut heather (B) and #891 misty olive (C)

■ One pair size 7 (4.5mm) needles *or size to obtain gauge*

■ Two size 7 (4.5mm) double-pointed needles (dpns)

■ Size G-6 (4mm) crochet hook

■ Two ½"/13mm four-hole cream buttons (for eyes)

■ ¾"/19mm copper bell
(**Note** Omit the bell for very young babies.)

■ 12" x 12"/30.5cm x 30.5cm knife-edge pillow form

■ Polyester fiberfill

■ Black sewing thread and sewing needle

■ Pins

Double moss stitch
(multiple of 4 sts)
Rows 1 and 2 *K2, p2; rep from * to end.
Rows 3 and 4 *P2, k2; rep from * to end.
Work rows 1–4 for double moss st.

Stripe pattern
Working in St st (k on RS, p on WS), *work 2 rows A, 2 rows B; rep from * (4 rows) for stripe pat.

Right head
Beg at nose, with A, cast on 7 sts.
Row (inc) 1 (RS) K1, M1, knit to last st, M1, k1—9 sts.
Row (inc) 2 (WS) P1, M1 p-st, purl to last st, M1 p-st, p1—11 sts.
Row 3 Rep row 1—13 sts.
Row 4 Purl.
Rows 5–8 Rep rows 3 and 4 twice—17 sts.
Row 9 Knit.
Row 10 Rep row 2—19 sts.
Row 11 Knit.
Row 12 Purl.
Row 13 Rep row 1—21 sts.
Row 14 Purl.
Row 15 Knit.
Row (inc) 16 (WS) Purl to last st, M1 p-st, p1—22 sts.
Rows 17 and 18 Rep rows 11 and 12.
Row (inc) 19 (RS) K1, M1, knit to end—23 sts.
Rows 20, 22, 24, 26 and 28 Purl.

Rows 21, 23, 25, 27 and 29 Knit.
Row (dec)30 (WS)P1, p2tog, purl to end—22 sts.
Row 31 Knit.
Row 32 Purl.
Row (dec) 33 (RS) Knit to last 3 sts, k2tog, k1—21 sts.
Row 34 Purl.
Row 35 Knit.
Rows 36–41 Rep rows 30–35—19 sts.
Rows 42–44 Rep rows 30–32—18 sts.
Row 45 Rep row 33—17 sts.
Row 46 Purl.
Rows 47–50 Rep rows 45 and 46 twice—15 sts.
Row 51 Knit.
Row 52 Rep row 30—14 sts.
Rows 53 and 55 Knit.
Rows 54 and 56 Purl.
Row 57 Knit. Bind off all sts purlwise for neck edge.

Left head
Beg at nose, with B, cast on 7 sts. Rep rows 1–15 same as for right head.
Row (inc) 16 (WS) P1, M1 p-st, purl to end—22 sts.
Rows 17 and 18 Rep rows 11 and 12 same as for right head.
Row (inc) 19 (RS) Knit to last st, M1, k1—23 sts.
Rows 20–29 Work same as for right head.
Row (dec) 30 (WS) Purl to last 3 sts, p2tog, p1—22 sts.
Row 31 Knit.

Gauge
20 sts and 26 rows to 4"/10cm over double moss st using size 7 (4.5mm) needles. *Take time to check gauge.*

Sheep Pillow

Row 32 Purl.
Row (dec) 33 (RS) K1, ssk, knit to end—21 sts.
Row 34 Purl.
Row 35 Knit.
Rows 36–41 Rep rows 30–35—19 sts.
Rows 42–44 Rep rows 30–32—18 sts.
Row 45 Rep row 33—17 sts.
Row 46 Purl.
Rows 47–50 Rep rows 45 and 46 twice—15 sts.
Row 51 Knit.
Row 52 Rep row 30—14 sts.
Rows 53–57 Work same as for right head. Bind off all sts purlwise for neck edge.

Right ear
Beg at bottom edge, with A, cast on 3 sts.
Row 1 (RS) Knit.
Row 2 Purl.
Row (inc) 3 (RS) K1, M1, knit to last st, M1, k1—5 sts.
Row 4 Purl.
Rows 5 and 6 Rep rows 3 and 4—7 sts.
Rows 7, 9, 11, 13 and 15 Knit.
Rows 8, 10, 12, 14 and 16 Purl.
Row (dec) 17 (RS) Ssk, knit to last 2 sts, k2tog—5 sts.
Row 18 Purl.
Row 19 Ssk, k1, k2tog—3 sts.
Cut yarn, leaving a 6"/15cm tail, and thread through rem sts. Pull tog tightly and secure end.

Left ear
Work same as right ear, using B.

Right body
Beg at bottom edge, with B, cast on 60 sts. Knit 1 row. Cont in double moss st until piece measures 12"/30.5cm from beg, end with a WS row. Bind off all sts knitwise

Left body
Work same as right body, using A.

Legs (make 4)
With C, cast on 13 sts. Work in garter st (knit *every* row) for 1"/2.5cm, end with a WS row. Cut C. Change to A and work in stripe pat for 6"/15cm, end with 2 rows B. Bind off knitwise using B.

Tail
With dpn and A, cast on 7 sts. Work in I-cord (see page 20) as foll:
*Next row (RS) With 2nd dpn, k7, do not turn. Slide sts back to beg of needle to work next row from RS; rep from * 8 times more.
Next (dec) row (RS) With 2nd dpn, k2tog, k3, k2tog, do not turn—5 sts. Slide sts back to beg of needle to work next row from RS.
Next (dec) row (RS) With 2nd dpn, k2tog, k1, k2tog—3 sts. Cut yarn, leaving an 8"/20.5cm tail, and thread through rem sts. Stuff lightly with fiberfill. Pull tog tightly and secure end.

Finishing
Lightly block body pieces to measure 12" x 12"/30.5cm x 30.5cm. Place head pieces tog, RS facing. Sew tog, leaving neck edges open; turn RS out. Fold each leg in half lengthwise, RS facing. Sew bottom, then long edges tog; turn RS out. Lightly steam seams.

EYES
Position each button eye 2¼"/5.5cm from neck edge and 1"/2.5cm from top seam. Using black thread, sew on button using cross stitches as shown in photo.

EARS
With RS of right ear facing and A, beg at bottom edge and embroider a row of chain stitches close to the outer edge, ending at opposite bottom edge. Rep for left ear using B. Fold bottom edge of right ear in half at bottom edge so WS are tog, then tack to secure. Position ear on right head so bottom edge is 1½"/4cm from neck edge and ¾"/2cm from top seam. Sew bottom edge in place. Rep for left ear and left head. Stuff head with fiberfill.

ASSEMBLING
Place right body RS up on work surface so cast-on edge is at bottom. Place head directly on top of right body with neck edge of head along RH edge of right body so top of neck is ½"/1.3cm from top edge of body and edge of neck is even with side edge of body; pin in place. Place left body WS up on top so cast-on edge is at bottom. Working through all thicknesses, sew head to body; remove pins.

Place on work surface again so right body is on bottom. Flip left body over toward the right. Place legs upside down and directly on top of right body so top edges of legs are even with cast-on edge of body. Space first leg ½"/1.3cm from side edge of body, second leg ¾"/2cm from first leg, fourth leg ½"/1.3cm from opposite side edge of body and third leg ¾"/2cm from fourth leg; pin in place. Flip left body back over right body. Working through all thicknesses, sew legs to body; remove pins. Sew top edges of bodies tog. Turn RS out. Insert pillow form. Sew rem edges closed. Sew tail to top back corner.

TIE
With crochet hook and C, crochet a 28"/71cm-long chain. Fasten off. Thread on bell. Knot ends of chain. Tie chain around neck. ■

Boatneck Pullover

Buttons along the shoulders of this cabled winner make for easy dressing.

DESIGNED BY THERESE CHYNOWETH

INTERMEDIATE

Sizes

Instructions are written for size 6 months. Changes for 12 and 18 months are in parentheses.

Knitted measurements

Chest 22 (24, 26)"/56 (61, 66)cm
Length 11 (12, 13)"/28 (30.5, 33)cm
Upper arm 9 (10, 11)"/23 (25.5, 28)cm

Materials

■ 2 (3, 3) 3½oz/100g balls (each approx 220yd/201m) of Cascade Yarns *220 Superwash* (superwash wool) in #1951 sapphire heather

■ One pair size 7 (4.5mm) needles *or size to obtain gauge*

■ Cable needle (cn)

■ Size E-4 (3.5mm) crochet hook

■ Stitch markers

■ Six ⅝"/16mm buttons

Stitch glossary

4-st RC Sl next 2 sts to cn and hold to *back*, k2, k2 from cn.
4-st LC Sl next 2 sts to cn and hold to *front*, k2, k2 from cn.

K1, p1 rib

(over a multiple of 2 sts plus 1)
Row 1 (RS) K1, *p1, k1; rep from * to end.
Row 2 P1, *k1, p1; rep from * to end.
Rep rows 1 and 2 for k1, p1 rib.

Back

Cast on 59 (65, 69) sts. Work in k1, p1 rib for 1¼"/3cm, end with a RS row. Purl next row.

BEG CHART PATS I, II AND III
Row 1 (RS) K1 (selvage st), pm, beg with st 6 (3, 1) of chart I and work to st 13, work 8-st rep once more, then work st 14, pm, work 23 sts of chart II, pm, beg with st 1 of chart III and work to st 9, work 8-st rep once more, work to st 0 (12, 14), pm, k1 (selvage st).
Keeping 1 selvage st each side in garter st (k every row), cont to foll charts in this way to row 8 for charts I and III, then rep rows 1–8 for pat sts, AT THE SAME TIME, work to row 4 for chart II, then rep rows 1–4 for cable pat.
Work even until piece measures 10 (11, 12)"/25.5 (28, 30.5)cm from beg, end with a WS row. Knit next row.
Beg with row 2, cont in k1, p1 rib for 1"/2.5cm. Bind off in rib.

Front

Work same as back. Sew a 3 (5, 6) st shoulder seam each side. Place markers 4½ (5, 5½)"/11.5 (12.5, 14)cm down from shoulders on back and fronts.

Gauges

19 sts and 28 rows to 4"/10cm over chart pats I, III and IV using size 7 (4.5mm) needles.
23 sts to 3¾"/9.5cm and 28 rows to 4"/10cm over chart pat II using size 7 (4.5mm) needles *Take time to check gauges.*

Boatneck Pullover

Sleeves

With RS facing, pick up and k 43 (47, 53) sts evenly spaced between markers. Purl next row.

BEG CHART PAT IV

Row 1 (RS) Beg with st 3 (1, 2) and work to st 12, work 8-st rep 4 (4, 5) times more, work to st 13 (15, 14). Cont to foll chart in this way to row 8, then rep rows 1–8 for pat st. AT THE SAME TIME, work even for 1"/2.5cm, end with a WS row. Dec 1 st each side on next row, then every 4th row 7 times more, then every other row 0 (1, 3) times—27 (29, 31) sts. Work even until piece measures 6 (6½, 7)"/15 (16.5, 17.5)cm from beg, end with a WS row. Knit next row. Beg with row 2, cont in k1, p1 rib for 1"/2.5cm. Bind off in rib.

Finishing

Block pieces to measurements.

Chart I

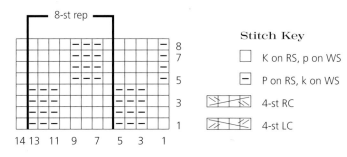

8-st rep

Stitch Key

☐ K on RS, p on WS

⊟ P on RS, k on WS

4-st RC

4-st LC

Chart II

23 sts

Chart III

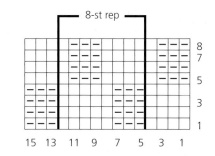

8-st rep

Chart IV

8-st rep

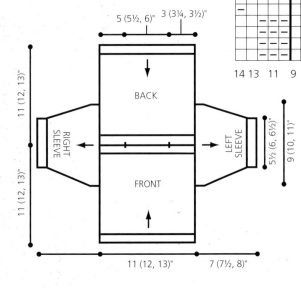

5 (5½, 6)"   3 (3¼, 3½)"

BACK

RIGHT SLEEVE   LEFT SLEEVE

FRONT

11 (12, 13)"

11 (12, 13)"

5½ (6, 6½)"

9 (10, 11)"

11 (12, 13)"   7 (7½, 8)"

BUTTON LOOPS

With RS of front facing, join yarn with a sl st in first free st after left shoulder seam, sl st in next st, *ch 4, skip next 2 sts, sl st in next 2 sts; rep from * twice more. Fasten off.
Skip center 25 (27, 29) sts, join yarn with a sl st in next st, then sl st in next st, *ch 4, skip next 2 sts, sl st in next 2 sts; rep from * twice more. Fasten off.
Sew side and sleeve seams.
Sew on buttons. ■

27

His and Hers Mittens

Mittens connected with I-cord will never get lost, even after hours of play in the snow!
No thumbs makes them super-quick to knit.

DESIGNED BY TANIS GRAY

EASY

Size

Instructions are written for size
6–12 months.

Knitted measurements

Hand circumference 5½"/14cm
Length of cuff approx 2"/5cm

Materials

▪ 1 3½oz/100g ball (approx 220yd/
201m) of Cascade Yarns *220
Superwash Quatro* (superwash wool) in
#1957 antigua (MC for boy's mitts) or
#1930 green tea (MC for girl's mitts)

▪ 1 3½oz/100g ball (approx 220yd/
201m) of Cascade Yarns *220
Superwash* (superwash wool) in #864
christmas green (CC for boy's mitts) or
#903 flamingo pink (CC for girl's mitts)

▪ One set (4) size 7 (4.5mm)
double-pointed needles (dpns) *or size
to obtain gauge*

▪ Stitch marker

Mitt (make 2)

CUFF

With dpn and CC, cast on 26 sts and
divide sts evenly over 3 needles. Join,
taking care not to twist sts on needles,
pm for beg of rnds. Work around in k1,
p1 rib for 2"/5cm. Cut CC.

HAND

With MC, work around in St st
(knit every rnd) until piece measures
5"/12.5cm from beg.

TOP SHAPING

Dec rnd 1 [K2tog] 13 times—13 sts.
Knit next rnd.
Dec rnd 2 [K2tog] 6 times, k1—7 sts.
Cut yarn, leaving a 6"/15cm tail, and
thread through rem sts. Pull tog tightly
and secure end.

I-cord

With RS facing, dpn and CC, pick up
and k 3 sts along bottom edge of cuff.
Work in I-cord (see page 20) as foll:
*Next row (RS) With 2nd dpn, k3, do
not turn. Slide sts back to beg of needle
to work next row from RS; rep from *
until I-cord measures 26"/66cm from beg
or same measurement as child's arm
span. Bind off; cut yarn, leaving a long
tail for sewing. Sew end of I-cord to
second mitt. ▪

Gauge

19 sts and 28 rnds to 4"/10cm over St st using size 7 (4.5mm) dpns.
Take time to check gauge.

28

Multicolored Stripes Blanket

Use up leftovers from your stash with this cheery, colorful throw. The visible stitching makes for an interesting design element.

DESIGNED BY JACQUELINE VAN DILLEN

Knitted measurements
Approx 29¾" x 27"/ 75.5cm x 68.5cm

Materials
■ 1 3½oz/100g ball (approx 220yd/201m) of Cascade Yarns *220 Superwash* (superwash wool) each in #802 green apple (A), #877 tangerine (B), #849 dark aqua (C), #886 citron (D), #815 black (E), #804 amethyst (F), #809 really red (G) and #883 puget sound (H)

■ One pair size 6 (4mm) needles *or size to obtain gauge*

■ Size G-6 (4mm) crochet hook

Strip #1
With A, cast on 54 sts. Cont in St st (knit on RS, purl on WS) and stripe sequence as foll:

6 rows A
6 rows B
6 rows C
8 rows D
2 rows E
6 rows F
2 rows D
2 rows E
4 rows G
36 rows C—10 stripes and 78 rows completed.

Cont stripe sequence as foll:
4 rows B
6 rows H
4 rows G
10 rows A
2 rows E
6 rows D
4 rows C
2 rows E
4 rows H
36 rows G—20 stripes and 156 rows completed.
Cont stripe sequence as foll:
4 rows E
8 rows B
4 rows D
8 rows F
2 rows E
6 rows H
4 rows G
2 rows E
4 rows C—29 stripes and 198 rows completed.
Bind off using C.

Gauge
22 sts and 30 rows to 4"/10cm over St st using size 6 (4mm) needles.
Take time to check gauge.

Multicolored Stripes Blanket

Strip #2
With F, cast on 54 sts.
Cont in St st and stripe
sequence as foll:
4 rows F
2 rows H
2 rows E
36 rows G—4 stripes and 44
rows completed.
Cont stripe sequence as foll:
4 rows B
6 rows D
6 rows B
4 rows E
2 rows G
4 rows A
4 rows H
2 rows E
4 rows F
36 rows A—14 stripes and 116
rows completed.
Cont stripe sequence as foll:
4 rows B
6 rows C
2 rows E
6 rows F
2 rows E
6 rows D
4 rows B
2 rows G
4 rows H
36 rows F—24 stripes and 188
rows completed.
Cont stripe sequence as foll:
2 rows C
4 rows B
4 rows D—27 stripes and 198
rows completed.
Bind off using D.

Strip #3
With H, cast on 54 sts.
Cont in St st and stripe
sequence as foll:
4 rows H
6 rows F
4 rows D
10 rows B
2 rows E
6 rows G
2 rows D
2 rows E
6 rows C
36 rows H—10 stripes and 78
rows completed.
Cont stripe sequence as foll:
4 rows A
6 rows G
6 rows B
8 rows C
2 rows F
6 rows E
4 rows F
2 rows C
4 rows B
36 rows D—20 stripes and 156
rows completed.
Cont stripe sequence as foll:
6 rows C
6 rows F
4 rows B
8 rows A
2 rows E
6 rows G
2 rows E
4 rows H
4 rows G—29 stripes and 198
rows completed.
Bind off using G.

Finishing
Block each strip so it measures
9¾" x 26½"/24.5cm x 67cm.
Sew strips tog (see photo on
page 81). Using F, embroider
a vertical line of cross stitches
over each seam as shown
in photo below.

EDGING
With RS facing and crochet hook,
join F with a sl st in any corner.
Rnd 1 (RS) Ch 1, working from
left to right, work in reverse sc
evenly around entire edge,
working 3 sc in each corner,
join rnd with a sl st in first sc.
Fasten off. ■

Pirate Hats

Arrrrr! These earflap caps are just the ticket when you're off to sea—or just to a playdate. They'll keep little ones warm no matter the conditions!

DESIGNED BY ERSSIE MAJOR

INTERMEDIATE

Size
Instructions are written for size 6 months.

Knitted measurements
Head circumference 15½"/39.5cm
Depth 6¾"/17cm (excluding earflaps)

Materials
- 1 3½oz/100g ball (approx 220yd/201m) of Cascade Yarns *220 Superwash* (superwash wool) each in:

TEAL HAT
- #810 teal (MC) and #910A winter white (CC)

RED HAT
- #893 ruby (MC) and #910A winter white (CC)

- Size 6 (4mm) circular needle, 16"/40cm length *or size to obtain gauge*

- One set (5) size 6 (4mm) double-pointed needles (dpns)

- Stitch marker

Note
To work in the rnd, always read charts from right to left.

Hat
With circular needle and MC, cast on 84 sts. Join and pm, taking care not to twist sts on needles.
Rnd 1 *K1, p1; rep from * around.
Rnd 2 K the purl sts and p the knit sts. Rep rnd 2 six times more. Cont in St st (knit every rnd) as foll:

BEG CHART PAT I
Rnd 1 Work 28-st rep of chart I three times. Cont to foll chart in this way to rnd 23. With MC only, cont to work even until piece measures 5"/12.5cm from beg.

CROWN SHAPING
Note Change to dpns (dividing sts evenly between 4 needles) when there are too few sts to work with circular needle.
Dec rnd 1 *K19, k2tog; rep from * around—80 sts.
Dec rnd 2 *K8, k2tog; rep from * around—72 sts.
Dec rnd 3 *K7, k2tog; rep from * around—64 sts.
Dec rnd 4 *K6, k2tog; rep from * around—56 sts.
Dec rnd 5 *K5, k2tog; rep from * around—48 sts.
Dec rnd 6 *K4, k2tog; rep from * around—40 sts.
Dec rnd 7 *K3, k2tog; rep from * around—32 sts.
Dec rnd 8 *K2, k2tog; rep from * around—24 sts.
Dec rnd 9 *K1, k2tog; rep from * around—16 sts.
Dec rnd 10 [K2tog] 8 times—8 sts. Cut yarn, leaving an 8"/20.5cm tail and thread through rem sts; do not secure end.

Gauge
22 sts and 28 rnds to 4"/10cm over St st and chart pat using size 6 (4mm) circular needle.
Take time to check gauge.

Pirate Hats

Right earflap

Position hat so RS is facing and cast-on edge is at top.

BEG CHART PAT II

Count 8 sts from rnd-joining, with dpns and MC, pick up and work 1 st in each of next 23 cast-on sts as foll:
Row 1 (RS) K1, p1, k1, pm, k17, pm, k1, p1, k1. Cont to foll chart with row 2 (WS) and work to row 14—13 sts.

EARFLAP SHAPING

Dec row 1 (RS) Work in seed st over first 3 sts, sl marker, ssk, knit to 2 sts before last marker, k2tog, sl marker, work in seed st over last 3 sts. Work next row even. Rep last 2 rows once more—9 sts.
Dec row 2 (RS) Work in seed st over first 3 sts, drop marker, SK2P, drop marker, work in seed st over last 3 sts—7 sts. Work next row even.
Dec row 3 (RS) K1, ssk, k1, k2tog, k1—5 sts. Work next row even.
Dec row 4 (RS) K1, ssk, k2—4 sts. Work next row even.

I-CORD TIE (see page 20)
*Next row (RS) With 2nd dpn, k4, do not turn. Slide sts back to beg of needle to work next row from RS; rep from * 23 times more. Cut yarn, leaving an 8"/20.5cm tail. Thread tail in tapestry needle, then thread through rem sts; do not secure end.

CHART I

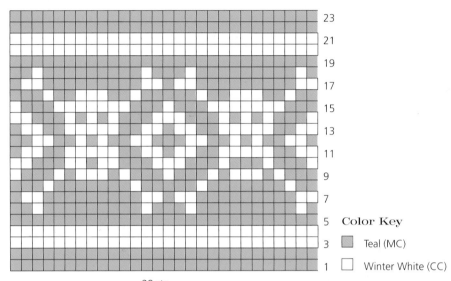

28 sts

Color Key

☐ Teal (MC)

☐ Winter White (CC)

CHART II

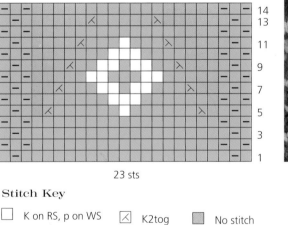

23 sts

Stitch Key

☐ K on RS, p on WS

⊟ P on RS, k on WS

◩ K2tog

◪ Ssk

☐ No stitch

Pirate Hats

CHART I

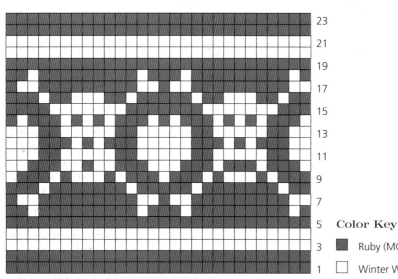

28 sts

CHART II

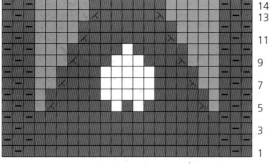

23 sts

Color Key

- ■ Ruby (MC)
- □ Winter White (CC)

Stitch Key

- □ K on RS, p on WS
- − P on RS, k on WS
- ⊠ K2tog
- ⊠ Ssk
- ▨ No stitch

Left earflap

Position hat so RS is facing and cast-on edge is at top.

BEG CHART PAT II
Count 22 sts from right earflap, with dpns and MC, pick up and work 1 st in each of next 23 cast-on sts as foll:
Row 1 (RS) K1, p1, k1, pm, k17, pm, k1, p1, k1. Cont to work same as right earflap.

Finishing

TWISTED CORD
Cut two 14"/35.5cm strands each of MC and CC. Put strands together and fold in half. Tie ends into a knot. Holding the knot in your hand, slip the loop over a hook and pull tight. Slip a pencil through the knotted end, then rotate the pencil, twisting the cord until it starts to double back on itself. Put one finger in center of cord and carefully fold in half, letting two ends of cord twist together. Tie an overhand knot at folded end, then tie another overhand knot 2"/5cm below it; trim off below this knot.

POMPOMS (make 3)
Using equal amounts of MC and CC, make three 1½"/3.5cm-diameter pompoms. Sew a pompom to end of each I-cord tie using I-cord tails. Sew a pompom to folded end of twisted cord. Insert opposite end of twisted cord into opening at top of hat. Pull hat tail tog tightly and secure end and twisted cord. ■

Lace-Edged Cardigan

Bold knitted stripes get the soft treatment with a filigree border in this vintage-inspired sweater.

DESIGNED BY LORNA MISER

INTERMEDIATE

Sizes

Instructions are written for size 3 months. Changes for 6 and 12 months are in parentheses.

Knitted measurements

Chest (closed) 20 (22, 24)"/51 (56, 61)cm
Length 9¼ (10¼, 11½)"/23.5 (26, 29)cm
Upper arm 8 (9, 10)"/20.5 (23, 25.5)cm

Materials

■ 1 (1, 1) 3½oz/100g ball (approx 220yd/201m) of Cascade Yarns *220 Superwash* (superwash wool) each in #902 soft pink (A) and #881 then there's mauve (B)

■ Contrasting worsted weight yarn (waste yarn)

■ One pair size 6 (4mm) needles *or size to obtain gauge*

■ Two size 5 (3.75mm) double-pointed needles (dpns) for I-cord ties

■ Size G-6 (4mm) crochet hook (for chain-st provisional cast-on)

■ Stitch holders

■ 2yd/2m cotton lace, ⅞"/22mm wide

Notes

1) Cardigan is made in one piece from bottom back edge to bottom front edges.
2) Sleeves are added with the chain-st provisional cast-on method.
3) First and last rows of sleeves are grafted tog using Kitchener stitch.

Stripe pattern

Working in St st, *work 4 rows A, 4 rows B; rep from * (8 rows) for stripe pat.

Cardigan

BACK
With straight needles and A, cast on 55 (61, 67) sts. Working in St st, cont in stripe pat until 10 (11, 12) stripes have been completed, end with a WS row.

BEG SLEEVES

With crochet hook and waste yarn, ch 27 (30, 33) for chain-st provisional cast-on. Cut yarn and draw end though lp on hook. Make another chain for left sleeve and set aside. With first chain, turn chain over so bottom lps are at top and cut end is at left.

Next row (RS) With free needle and next color, beg 2 lps from right end, pick up and k 1 st in each of next 22 (25, 28) lps, k55 (61, 67) sts of back, then beg 2 lps from right end of 2nd chain, pick up and k 1 st in each of next 22 (25, 28) lps—99 (111,123) sts.
Work even until 7 (8, 9) sleeve stripes have been completed. With next color, work even for 2 rows.

BACK NECK SHAPING

Next row (RS) K 36 (42,48) sts, join a 2nd ball of same color and bind off center 27 sts, knit to end. Working both sides at once, purl next row. Change to next color and work even for 4 rows.

FRONT NECK SHAPING

Change to next color and inc 1 st at each neck edge on next row, then every other row once more, end with a WS row (4 rows completed). Change to next color and inc 1 st at neck edge on next row,

Gauge

22 sts and 30 rows to 4"/10cm over St st (knit on RS, purl on WS) using size 6 (4mm) needles.
Take time to check gauge.

Lace-Edged Cardigan

then *every* row once more (2 rows completed).

With same color, cast on 9 sts at each neck edge once—49 (55, 61) sts each side (4 rows completed). Change to next color.

Work even until 14 (16, 18) sleeve stripes have been completed, end with a WS row. Change to next color and work even for 3 rows, end with a RS row.

END SLEEVES
Next row (WS) With first ball of yarn, p 22 (25, 28) sts, place these sts on holder, p 27 (30, 33) sts; with 2nd ball of yarn, p 27 (30, 33) sts, place rem 22 (25, 28) sts on holder. Change to next color. Work even until 10 (11, 12) stripes more have been completed, end with a WS row. Bind off each side knitwise.

Finishing
Block piece to measurements.

JOINING SLEEVES
Wth RS facing, release cut end from lp of waste yarn chain. Pulling out 1 ch at a time, place live sts from cast-on to a needle, then place sts on holder on a needle. Graft first row of sts to last row of sts using Kitchener stitch. Rep for rem sleeve. Sew side seams.

NECKBAND
With RS facing, straight needles and A, pick up and k 17 sts along right front neck edge, 27 sts along back neck edge, then 17 sts along left front neck edge—61 sts. Knit next row. Bind off all sts knitwise.

TIES
With RS facing, dpns and A, pick up and k 4 sts along side edge of right front neckband. Work in I-cord (see p. 20) as foll:
Next row (RS) With 2nd dpn, k4, do not turn. Slide sts back to beg of needle to work next row from RS; rep from * until I-cord measures 9½"/24cm from beg. Cut yarn, leaving a 6"/15cm tail, and thread through rem sts. Pull tog tightly and secure end. Work a 2nd tie in side edge of left front neckband.

LACE TRIM
Using a continuous length of lace, fold cut edge ¼"/5mm over to WS, butt fold against bottom edge of right front neckband so edge of lace is even with right front edge; pin. Taking care to maintain st and row gauge, cont to pin lace down right front to bottom edge, fold a mitered corner, pin, then cont along bottom edge to left front. Fold a mitered corner, pin, then cont to pin lace up left front to neckband. Cut lace, leaving enough for a ¼"/5mm fold-over to butt against bottom edge of left front neckband. Fold edge ¼"/5mm over to WS and pin. Machine-stitch or hand-stitch lace in place along each edge.

For cuffs, cut two pieces of lace 1½"/4cm longer than circumference around cuff edge. Beg at underarm, pin lace around cuff so edge of lace is even with cuff edge. Fold free end of lace ½"/1.3cm to WS, then lap this end over the opposite end. Machine-stitch or hand-stitch lace in place along each edge and along fold. Lightly steam-press lace trim. ■

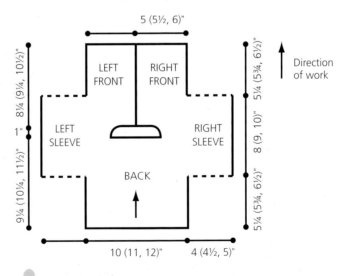

5 (5½, 6)"

8¼ (9¼, 10½)"

5¼ (5¾, 6½)"

LEFT FRONT

RIGHT FRONT

Direction of work

1"

LEFT SLEEVE

RIGHT SLEEVE

8 (9, 10)"

9¼ (10¼, 11½)"

BACK

5¼ (5¾, 6½)"

10 (11, 12)"   4 (4½, 5)"

Quick Tip
Adding purchased lace is an easy way to dress up a simple knit. Try ribbon for a different look.

Seed Stitch Yoke Cardi

A cheery color and bodice detailing
dress up this basic raglan sweater.

DESIGNED BY NICHOLE REESE

INTERMEDIATE

Sizes
Instructions are written for size 3 months. Changes for 6 and 12 months are in parentheses.

Knitted measurements
Chest (closed) 19½ (21½, 23½)"/49.5 (54.5, 59.5)cm
Length 10½ (11½, 12½)"/26.5 (29, 31.5)cm
Upper arm 7 (8, 9)"/18 (20.5, 23)cm

Materials
■ 2 (3, 3) 3½oz/100g balls (each approx 220yd/201m) of Cascade Yarns *220 Superwash Quatro* (superwash wool) in #1932 butterscotch

■ Size 7 (4.5mm) circular needle, 32"/81cm length *or size to obtain gauge*

■ One pair size 7 (4.5mm) needles

■ One set (5) size 7 (4.5mm) double-pointed needles (dpns)

■ Size G-6 (4mm) crochet hook

■ Stitch holders

■ Stitch markers

■ Five ½"/13mm buttons

Notes
1) Body and yoke are worked back and forth in one piece from the bottom up.
2) Sleeves are worked in the round.

Stitch glossary
M1 Insert LH needle from back to front under the strand between last st worked and the next st on the LH needle. Knit into the front loop to twist the st.

Seed Stitch
(over an odd number of sts)
Row 1 (RS) K1, *p1, k1; rep from * to end.
Row 2 K the purl sts and p the knit sts. Rep row 2 for seed st.

Sleeves (make 2)
With dpn, cast on 32 (34, 36) sts and divide sts evenly over 4 needles. Join, taking care not to twist sts on needles, pm for beg of rnds.
Rnd 1 *K1, p1; rep from * around.
Rnds 2–4 K the purl sts and p the knit sts.
Rnds 5 and 7 Knit.
Rnds 6 and 8 Purl. Cont in St st (knit every rnd) for 10 (6, 4) rnds.
Inc rnd K1, M1, knit to 1 st before marker, M1, k1. Rep inc rnd every 16th (12th, 8th) rnd 1 (2, 4) times more—

36 (40, 46) sts. Work even until piece measures 6½ (7, 7½)"/16.5 (18, 19)cm from beg, end 4 sts before rnd marker.
Next rnd K8 dropping marker, place these 8 sts on holder for underarm, knit to end of rnd. Place rem 28 (32, 38) sts on holder for sleeve. Set aside.

Body
With circular needle, cast on 93 (103, 113) sts. Work in seed st for 4 rows, then work in garter st (knit every row) for 4 rows. Cont in St st and work even until piece measures 5½ (6, 6½)"/14 (15, 16.5)cm from beg, end with a WS row.

Yarn Smarts
Superwash wool is washable, of course, but it's a good idea to use a gentle detergent formulated for babies to avoid irritating delicate skin.

Gauge
20 sts and 27 rows to 4"/10cm over St st using size 7 (4.5mm) circular needle. *Take time to check gauge.*

Seed Stitch Yoke Cardi

YOKE

Next row (RS) K 18 (20, 23) sts, sl next 8 sts to holder for right underarm, k 28 (32, 38) sts from holder for right sleeve, k 41 (47, 51) sts for back, sl next 8 sts to holder for left underarm, k 28 (32, 38) sts from holder for left sleeve, k 18 (20, 23) sts - 133 (151, 173) sts. Beg with a purl row, cont in St st for 5 (9, 13) rows. Work in garter st for 4 rows, then work in seed st for 6 rows.

Dec row 1 (RS) K 3 (4, 3), *k2tog, k2; rep from *, end k 2 (3, 2)—101 (115, 131) sts. Work in garter st for 3 rows, then work in seed st for 6 rows.

Dec row 2 (RS) K 3 (4, 3), *k2tog, k1; rep from *, end k 2 (3, 2)—69 (79, 89) sts. Work in garter st for 3 rows, then work in seed st for 6 rows.

Dec row 3 (RS) K1, *k1, [k2tog] twice; rep from *, end k2tog, k1—42 (48, 54) sts. Work in garter st for 3 rows. Bind off all sts knitwise.

Finishing

Block piece to measurements. Graft underarm sts tog using Kitchener stitch.

BUTTON BAND

With RS facing and straight needles, pick up and k 53 (57, 63) sts evenly spaced along left front edge. Work in garter st for 3 rows, then work in seed st for 4 rows. Bind off in seed st. Place markers for 5 buttons on button band, with the first ½"/1.3cm from lower edge, the last ¾"/2cm from neck edge and the others evenly spaced between.

BUTTONHOLE BAND

With RS facing and straight needles, pick up and k 53 (57, 63) sts evenly spaced along right front edge. Work in garter st for 3 rows, then work in seed st for 1 row.
Next (buttonhole) row (WS) *Work in seed st to marker, bind off next 2 sts; rep from * 4 times more, work in seed st to end.
Next row Work in seed st, casting on 2 sts over bound-off sts. Cont in seed st for 1 row more. Bind off in seed st.

NECK EDGING

With RS facing and crochet hook, join yarn with a sl st in right neck edge.
Row 1 (RS) Sl st in each st across. Fasten off. Sew on buttons. ■

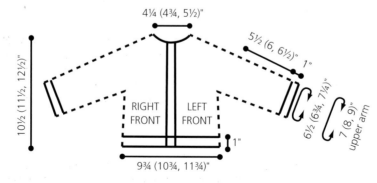

Ram's Horn Hat

This wool cap is extra "woolly" with an adorable horn design on either side!
A turned brim keeps the bottom edge neat and flat.

DESIGNED BY MELISSA HALVORSON

EXPERIENCED

Size
Instructions are written for size
6–12 months.

Knitted measurements
Head circumference 16"/40.5cm
Depth 6¾"/17cm

Materials
■ 1 3½oz/100g ball (approx 220yd/
201m) of Cascade Yarns *220
Superwash* (superwash wool) each
in #868 autumn heather (MC) and
#910A winter white (CC)

■ Size 7 (4.5mm) circular needle,
16"/40cm length *or size to obtain gauge*

■ One set (5) size 7 (4.5mm)
double-pointed needles (dpns)

■ Stitch markers

Note
To work in the rnd, always read charts
from right to left.

Hat
With circular needle and MC, cast on 68
sts. Join and pm, taking care not to twist
sts on needle. Work around in St st (knit
every rnd) for 1"/2.5cm. Purl next rnd for
turning ridge. Cont in St st for 8 rnds.

Gauges
17 sts and 18 rnds to 4"/10cm over St st using size 7 (4.5mm) circular needle.
20 sts and 24 rnds to 4"/10cm over St st and chart pat using size 7 (4.5mm) circular needle.
Take time to check gauges.

Ram's Horn Hat

Chart I

22
21
19
17
15
13
11
9
7
5
3
1

30 sts

Chart II

22
21
19
17
15
13
11
9
7
5
3
1

30 sts

BEG CHART PATS

Rnd 1 K2 with MC, pm, work 30 sts of chart I, pm, k4 with MC, pm, work 30 sts of chart II, pm, k2 with MC. Cont to foll charts in this way to rnd 22, removing all but rnd marker on last rnd. Cont with MC only.

CROWN SHAPING

Note Change to dpns (dividing sts evenly between 4 needles) when there are too few sts to work with circular needle.
Dec rnd 1 *K32, k2tog; rep from * around—66 sts.
Dec rnd 2 *K4, k2tog; rep from * around—55 sts.
Dec rnd 3 *K3, k2tog; rep from * around—44 sts.
Dec rnd 4 *K2, k2tog; rep from * around—33 sts.
Dec rnd 5 *K1, k2tog; rep from * around—22 sts.
Dec rnd 6 [K2tog] 11 times—11 sts.
Cut yarn, leaving an 8"/20.5cm tail and thread through rem sts. Pull tog tightly and secure end.

Finishing

Turn bottom edge of hat to WS along turning ridge and sew in place. ■

Color Key

■ Autumn Heather (MC)

☐ Winter White (CC)

33 Overalls

Overalls are great for layering. Buttons up the legs
make them easy to get on and off.

DESIGNED BY LORI STEINBERG

INTERMEDIATE

Sizes
Instructions are written for size 6 months.
Changes for 12 and 18 months are in
parentheses.

Knitted measurements
Chest/Waist
21 (22, 23)"/53.5 (56, 58.5)cm
Length
21 (23, 25)"/53.5 (58.5, 63.5)cm
Inseam
8 (9, 10)"/20.5 (23, 25.5)cm

Materials
■ 2 (3, 3) 3½oz/100g balls (each approx
220yd/201m) of Cascade Yarns *220
Superwash* (superwash wool) in #897
baby denim (A)

■ 1 ball each in #819 chocolate (B) and
#906 chartreuse (C)

■ One pair size 7 (4.5mm) needles *or size
to obtain gauge*

■ Size G-6 (4mm) crochet hook

■ Stitch holder

■ 8 (10, 10) ⅝"/16mm buttons

Stitch glossary
kf&b Inc 1 by knitting into the front and
back of the next st.

Narrow stripe pattern
Rows 1 and 2 With B, knit.
Row 3 With A, knit.
Row 4 With A, purl.
Rep rows 1–4 for narrow stripe pat.

Medium stripe pattern
Rows 1 and 2 With B, knit.
Rows 3 and 5 With A, knit.
Rows 4 and 6 With A, purl.
Rep rows 1–6 for medium stripe pat.

Wide stripe pattern
Rows 1 and 2 With B, knit.
Rows 3, 5 and 7 With A, knit.
Rows 4, 6 and 8 With A, purl.
Rep rows 1–8 for wide stripe pat.

Back
LEFT LEG
With C, cast on 20 (22, 24) sts. Work in
garter st (knit every row) for 10 rows.
Cont on narrow stripe pat and work even
for 8 rows. Cont in narrow stripe pat,
work as foll:
Next (inc) row (RS) K1, kf&b, k to end.
Rep inc row every 8th (10th, 12th) row
5 times more—26 (28, 30) sts. Work

even until piece measures 8 (9, 10)"/20.5
(23, 25.5)cm from beg, end with a row 4.
Cut yarn and place sts on holder.

RIGHT LEG
With C, cast on 20 (22, 24) sts. Work in
garter st (knit every row) for 10 rows.
Cont in narrow stripe pat and work even
for 8 rows. Cont in narrow stripe pat,
work as foll:
Next (inc) row (RS) Knit to last 2 sts,
kf&b, k1. Rep inc row every 8th (10th,
12th) row 5 times more—26 (28, 30) sts.
Work even until piece measures same
length as left leg, end with a row 4.

JOINING
Cont in narrow stripe pat, work as foll:
Next row (RS) With B knit 26 (28, 30)
sts, then knit 26 (28, 30) sts from
holder—52 (56, 60) sts. Work even until
piece measures approx 1¾ (2¼, 2¾)"/4.5
(5.5, 7)cm from joining, end with a row
4. Change to medium stripe pat and rep
rows 1–6 three times. Change to wide
stripe pat and rep rows 1–8 twice, then
rep rows 1 and 2 once. Cont with A only
and work even in St st until piece
measures 8 (8½, 9)"/20.5 (21.5, 23)cm
from joining, end with a WS row.

Gauge
20 sts and 34 rows to 4"/10cm over narrow stripe pat using size 7 (4.5mm) needles. *Take time to check gauge.*

Overalls

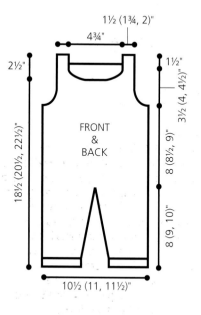

FRONT & BACK

1½ (1¾, 2)"

4¾"

2½"

1½"

3½ (4, 4½)"

18½ (20½, 22½)"

8 (8½, 9)"

8 (9, 10)"

10½ (11, 11½)"

ARMHOLE SHAPING
Bind off 4 (5, 5) sts at beg of next 2 rows. Dec 1 st from each side on next row, then every other row 1 (1, 2) times more—40 (42, 44) sts. Work even until armhole measures 3½ (4, 4½)"/9 (10, 11.5)cm, end with a WS row.

NECK SHAPING
Next row (RS) K 8 (9, 10), join a 2nd ball of A and bind off center 24 sts, knit to end. Working both sides at once, work even on 8 (9, 10) sts each side until armhole measures 5 (5½, 6)"/12.5 (14, 15)cm, end with WS row. Bind off each side for shoulders.

Front
Work same as back until armhole measures 2½ (3, 3½)"/6.5 (7.5, 9)cm, end with a WS row.

NECK SHAPING
Next row (RS) K 17 (18, 19), join a 2nd ball of A and bind off center 6 sts, knit to end. Working both sides at once, bind off 5 sts from each neck edge once, then 2 sts twice—8 (9, 10) sts each side. Work even until armhole measures same as back to shoulder. Bind off each side for shoulders.

Finishing
Lightly block to measurements. Sew side seams. Sew left shoulder seam.

NECK EDGING
With RS facing and B, pick up and k 42 sts evenly spaced along back neck edge to left shoulder, pick up and k 56 sts evenly spaced along front neck edge—98

sts. Knit next row. Bind off all sts purlwise. Sew right shoulder seam.

ARMHOLE EDGING
With RS facing and crochet hook, join A with a sl st in side seam.
Rnd 1 Ch 1, making sure that work lies flat, sc evenly around armhole edge, join rnd with a sl st in first sc. Fasten off.

BUTTONBAND
With RS facing and crochet hook, join A with a sl st in side edge of first row of left back leg.
Row 1 (RS) Making sure that work lies flat, sl st evenly along left back leg to crotch, then along entire right back leg. Turn.
Row 2 Ch 1, half double crochet (hdc) in each st across. Turn.
Row 3 Ch 1, hdc in each st across. Fasten off. Place markers for 4 (5, 5) buttons along each side of button band, with the first ½"/1.3cm from lower edge, the next 2"/5cm from lower edge, the last 1"/2.5cm from joining and the other 1 (2, 2) evenly spaced between.

BUTTONHOLE BAND
With RS facing and crochet hook, join A with a sl st in side edge of first row of right front leg.
Row 1 (RS) Making sure that work lies flat, sl st evenly along right front leg to crotch, then along entire left front leg. Turn.
Row 2 Ch 1, *hdc to marker, ch 2, skip next st; rep from * 3 (4, 4) times more, hdc in each st to end. Turn.
Row 3 Ch 1, hdc in each st across, working 1 hdc in each ch-2 sp. Fasten off. Sew on buttons. ■

Lace Sampler Blanket

This sumptuous blanket is made up of a number of lovely lace patterns.

DESIGNED BY LORETTA DACHMAN

INTERMEDIATE

Knitted measurements
Approx 35" x 42"/89cm x 106.5cm

Materials
■ 6 3½oz/100g balls (each approx 220yd/201m) of Cascade Yarns *220 Superwash* (superwash wool) in #839 medium rose

■ Size 7 (4.5mm) circular needle, 36"/91cm length *or size to obtain gauge*

■ Stitch markers

Stitch glossary
M1 Insert LH needle from back to front under the strand between last st worked and the next st on the LH needle. Knit into the front loop to twist the st.

Blanket
Cast on 176 sts. Work in garter st (knit every row) for 17 rows, end with a RS row.
Next row (WS) K9, pm, purl to last 9 sts, pm, k9.

BEG CHART PATS
Row 1 (RS) K9, sl marker, work chart 1 over next 14 sts, pm, work chart 2 over next 52 sts, pm, work chart 3 over next 26 sts, pm, work chart 2 over next 52 sts, pm, work chart 4 over next 14 sts, k9. Keeping 9 sts each side in garter st, cont to work charts in this way to row 12, then rep rows 1–12 twenty-one times more.
Next row (RS) Knit, dropping all markers. Cont in garter st for 16 rows more. Bind off all sts knitwise.

Finishing
Block piece lightly to measurements. ■

Gauge
20 sts and 28 rows to 4"/10cm over St st (k on RS, p on WS) using size 7 (4.5mm) circular needle. *Take time to check gauge.*

99

Lace Sampler Blanket

Chart I

Stitch Key

☐	K on RS, p on WS
⟋	K2tog
⟍	Ssk
O	Yo
M	M1

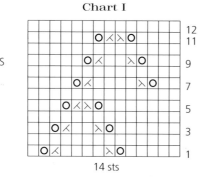

12
11
9
7
5
3
1

14 sts

Chart II

13 sts   13 sts   13 sts   13 sts

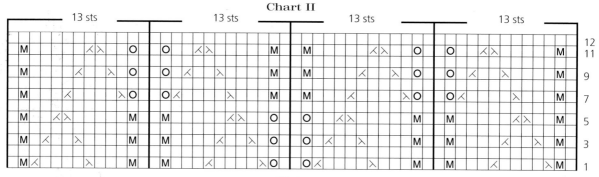

12
11
9
7
5
3
1

52 sts

Chart III

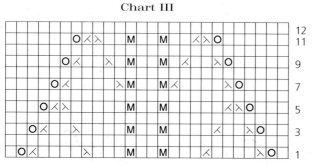

12
11
9
7
5
3
1

26 sts

Chart IV

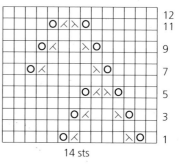

12
11
9
7
5
3
1

14 sts

Porcupine Blanket

Prickly animals become soft furry friends in this adorable throw!
Use it to keep baby warm or to decorate the nursery.

DESIGNED BY AMY BAHRT

EXPERIENCED

Knitted measurements
Approx 28" x 30"/71cm x 76cm

Materials
- 3 3½oz/100g balls (each approx 220yd/201m) of Cascade Yarns *220 Superwash* (superwash wool) in #900 charcoal (A)
- 2 balls in #1946 silver grey (B)
- 1 ball each in #1919 turtle (C), #910A winter white (D) and #1918 shire (E)
- 36"/91.5cm of sportweight or DK weight yarn in orange
- Size 7 (4.5mm) circular needle, 36"/91cm length *or size to obtain gauge*
- Size G-6 (4mm) crochet hook
- Bobbins
- Stitch markers
- Tapestry needle for embroidery

Notes
1) Use a separate bobbin (or strand) of color for each color section except for the porcupine legs, where you can carry colors across WS.
2) When changing colors, pick up

new color from under dropped color to prevent holes.
3) When working stripe pats, carry color not in use loosely up side edge.

Stripe pattern I
Working in St st, *work 4 rows B, 4 rows A; rep from * (8 rows) for stripe pat I.

Stripe pattern II
Working in St st, *work 2 rows A, 2 rows B; rep from * (4 rows) for stripe pat II.

Stripe pattern III
Working in St st, *work 4 rows A, 4 rows B; rep from * (8 rows) for stripe pat III.

Seed stitch stripe
Row 1 (RS) Knit.
Row 2 K1, *p1, k1; rep from * to end.
Rows 3–5 K the purl sts and p the knit sts.
Row 6 Purl.
Work rows 1–6 for seed st stripe.

Blanket
Note Work first and last 5 sts of every row in garter st using A. Work stripe pat and chart over center 127 sts.
With circular needle and A, cast on 137 sts. Work in garter st (knit every row) for 8 rows, end with a WS row.

BOTTOM PORCUPINE
Next row (RS) K5 with A, pm, work row 1 of stripe pat I to last 5 sts, pm, k5 with A.
Next row K5 with A, sl marker, work row 2 of stripe pat I to last 5 sts, sl marker, k5 with A.
Keeping 5 sts each side in garter st using A, cont to work center 127 sts in stripe pat I until 6 stripes have been completed. Change to B and work even for 2 rows. Change to C and work rows 1–6 of seed st stripe.

BEG CHART PAT
Row 1 (RS) K5 with A, sl marker, k88 with B, work 25 sts of chart, k14 with B, sl marker, k5 with A.
Cont to foll chart in this way to row 22. Keeping 5 sts each side in garter st using A, cont to work center 127 sts in St st using B for 4 rows.

CENTER PORCUPINE
Keeping 5 sts each side in garter st using A, work center 127 sts in stripe pat II until 12 stripes have been completed. Change to C and work rows 1–6 of seed st stripe.

BEG CHART PAT
Row 1 (RS) K5 with A, sl marker, k51

Gauge
20 sts and 26 rows to 4"/10cm over St st using size 7 (4.5mm) circular needle.
Take time to check gauge.

Porcupine Blanket

35

Color Key

- ▓ Charcoal (A)
- ▒ Silver Grey (B)
- ☐ Winter White (D)

Stitch Key

- ● French Knot

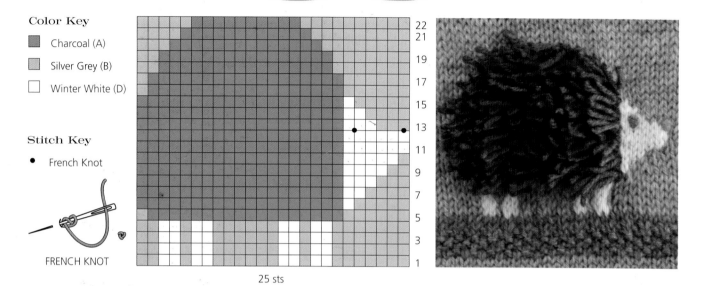

FRENCH KNOT

25 sts

with B, work 25 sts of chart, k51 with B, sl marker, k5 with A.
Cont to foll chart in this way to row 22. Keeping 5 sts each side in garter st using A, cont to work center 127 sts in St st using B for 4 rows.

TOP PORCUPINE

Keeping 5 sts each side in garter st using A, work center 127 sts in stripe pat III until 5 stripes have been completed. Change to B and work in St st for 2 rows. Change to C and work rows 1–6 of seed st stripe.

BEG CHART PAT

Row 1 (RS) K5 with A, sl marker, k15 with B, work 25 sts of chart, k87 with B, sl marker, k5 with A.
Cont to foll chart in this way to row 22. Keeping 5 sts each side in garter st using A, cont to work center 127 sts in St st

using B for 4 rows, then work stripe pat II until 12 stripes have been completed, dropping st markers on last row. With A only, work in garter st on all sts for 7 rows. Bind off all sts loosely knitwise.

Finishing

Block piece to measurements.

EYES

Using C, embroider a French knot eye where indicated on chart.

NOSES

Using orange, embroider a French knot nose where indicated on chart.

QUILLS

Cut 3"/7.5cm-long strands of A. With crochet hook, and working from left to right, attach fringe vertically in every other column of sts and every 3rd row of

porcupine body. Tie each strand close to blanket to secure. Trim fringe evenly.

LEAVES (make 9)

With dpn and E, cast on 3 sts.
Work in I-cord as foll:

*Next row (RS)** With 2nd dpn, k3, do not turn. Slide sts back to beg of needle to work next row from RS; rep from * twice more, inc 1 st each side of last row—5 sts.
Work back and forth on two dpns as foll:
Row 1 (RS) K2, yo, k1, yo, k2—7 sts.
Row 2 and all WS rows Purl.
Row 3 K3, yo, k1, yo, k3—9 sts.
Row 5 Ssk, k5, k2tog—7 sts.
Row 7 Ssk, k3, k2tog—5 sts.
Row 9 Ssk, k1, k2tog—3 sts.
Row 11 SK2P—1 st. Fasten off last st.
Sew leaves to seed st stripes as shown in photo. ■

36 Heart Hat

Show her how much you care with this loveable cap. The pockets on either side make it spunky and irresistible!

DESIGNED BY ANASTASIA BLAES

Size
Instructions are written for size 6–12 months.

Knitted measurements
Head circumference 16"/40.5cm
Depth 6"/15cm

Materials
■ 1 3½oz/100g ball (approx 220yd/201m) of Cascade Yarns *220 Superwash* (superwash wool) each in #1941 salmon (MC) and #1940 peach (CC)

■ One set (5) size 7 (4.5mm) double-pointed needles (dpns) *or size to obtain gauge*

■ One pair size 7 (4.5mm) needles

■ Stitch marker

Hat
With dpn and MC, cast on 84 sts, dividing sts evenly over 4 needles. Join and pm, taking care not to twist sts on needles.

BRIM
Rnd 1 Knit.
Rnd 2 Purl.
Rnd 3 Knit.
Rnd 4 *K14, p14; rep from * around twice more.
Rnds 5–22 Rep rnds 3 and 4.
Rnd 23 Knit.
Rnd 24 Purl.

SIDES
Rnd 1 K around.
Rnd 2 *K13, p1; rep from * around.
Rnds 3–6 Rep rnds 1 and 2.

CROWN SHAPING
Rnd (dec) 1 *K12, k2tog; rep from * around—78 sts.
Rnd 2 *K12, p1; rep from * around.
Rnd (dec) 3 *K11, k2tog; rep from * around—72 sts.
Rnd 4 *K11, p1; rep from * around.
Rnd (dec) 5 *K10, k2tog, rep from * around—66 sts.
Rnd 6 *K10, p1; rep from * around.
Rnd (dec) 7 *K9, k2tog; rep from * around—60 sts.
Rnd 8 *K9, p1; rep from * around.
Rnd (dec) 9 *K8, k2tog; rep from * around—54 sts.
Rnd 10 *K8, p1; rep from * around.
Rnd (dec) 11 *K7, k2tog; rep from * around—48 sts.

Gauge
22 sts and 28 rnds to 4"/10cm over St st using size 7 (4.5mm) dpns.
Take time to check gauge.

Heart Hat

Rnd 12 *K7, p1; rep from * around.
Rnd (dec) 13 *K6, k2tog; rep from * around—42 sts.
Rnd 14 *K6, p1; rep from * around.
Rnd (dec) 15 *K5, k2tog; rep from * around—36 sts.
Rnd 16 *K5, p1; rep from * around.
Rnd (dec) 17 *K4, k2tog; rep from * around—30 sts.
Rnd 18 *K4, p1; rep from * around.
Rnd (dec) 19 *K3, p2tog; rep from * around—24 sts.
Rnd (dec) 20 *K2, k2tog, rep from * around—18 sts.
Rnd (dec) 21 *K1, p2tog, rep from * around—12 sts
Rnd (dec) 22 [K2tog] 6 times—6 sts.
Cut yarn, leaving an 8"/20.5cm tail, and thread through rem sts. Pull tog tightly and secure end.

Heart pockets (make 3)
With straight needles and CC, cast on 16 sts. Knit next row.

BEG CHART PAT
Row 1 (RS) K1, work 14 sts of chart, k1.
Row 2 K1, work 14 sts of chart, k1.
Keeping 1 st each side in garter st (knit every row), cont to foll chart in this way to row 22.
Next row (RS) Purl. Bind off all sts knitwise.

Finishing
Place a heart pocket on top of a St st square on hat brim. Pocket will overlap slightly, with garter sts on each side of pocket and align with first and last row of garter st on top and bottom of St st square. Using CC, whipstitch along sides and bottom edges, leaving top open to form patch pocket. Rep for two rem pockets. ■

Color Key

☐ Salmon (MC)

■ Peach (CC)

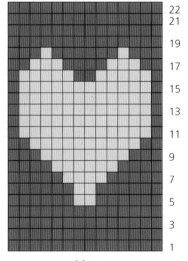

14 sts

37

Gator Sweater

Little reptile lovers will delight in this pullover with a knitted
and appliquéd alligator that wraps around the body.

DESIGNED BY TONIA BARRY

Sizes

Instructions are written for size 3 months.
Changes for 6 and 12 months are in
parentheses.

Finished measurements

- **Chest** 18 (20, 22)"/45.5 (51, 56)cm
- **Length** 10½ (11¾, 12¾)"/26.5
(30, 32.5)cm
- **Upper arm** 7 (8, 9)"/18 (20.5, 23)cm

Materials

■ 2 (3, 3) 3½oz/100g balls (each approx
220yd/201m) of Cascade Yarns *220
Superwash* (superwash wool) in #812
turquoise (MC)

■ 1 3½oz/100g hank (approx
437yd/400m) of Cascade Yarns *Heritage*
(superwash wool/nylon) each in #5629
citron (A) and #5641 mango (B)

■ Size 7 (4.5mm) circular needles,
16"/41cm and 24"/61cm long, *or size
to obtain gauge*

■ One set (5) size 7 (4.5mm)
double-pointed needles (dpns)

■ Stitch holders

■ Stitch markers

■ One ⅞"/22mm button (optional, for eye)

Note

Sweater is made in one piece from
the bottom up.

Sleeves

With dpns and MC, cast on 30 (32, 34) sts
and divide sts evenly over 4 needles. Join,
taking care not to twist sts on needles, pm
for beg of rnds. Work around in St st (knit
every rnd) for 1"/2.5cm.
Inc rnd K1, M1 (see page 4), knit to 1 st
before marker, M1, k1. Rep inc rnd every
18th (10th, 8th) rnd 2 (4, 6) times more—
36 (42, 48) sts. Work even until piece
measures 7½ (8, 9)"/19 (20.5, 23)cm from
beg, end 4 sts before rnd marker.
Next rnd K8 dropping marker, place these
8 sts on scrap yarn for underarm, knit to
end of rnd. Place rem 28 (34, 40) sts on
holder for sleeve. Set aside.

Body

With longer circular needle and MC, cast
on 96 (106, 116) sts. Join, taking care not
to twist sts on needle, pm for beg of rnds.
Work around in St st until piece measures
6 (6½, 7)"/15 (16.5, 18)cm from beg, end
last rnd 4 sts before rnd marker.
Next rnd K8 dropping marker, place these
8 sts on scrap yarn for underarm, knit until
there are 48 (53, 58) sts on RH needle,
place last 8 sts on scrap yarn for underarm,

knit to end of rnd—40 (45, 50) sts for
back and 40 (45, 50) sts for front.

YOKE

Next rnd K 28 (34, 40) sts from first sleeve
holder, pm, k 40 (45, 50) sts for front, pm,
k 28 (34, 40) sts from 2nd sleeve holder,
pm, k 40 (45, 50) sts for back, pm for beg
of rnds—136 (158, 180) sts. Work even
for 4 rnds. Change to shorter circular
needle when there are too few sts to work
with longer circular needle.
Dec rnd *K1, ssk, knit to 3 sts before next
marker, k2tog, k1, sl marker; rep from *
around 3 times more. Work next rnd even.
Rep last 2 rnds 9 (11, 13) times more—56
(62, 68) sts.

COLLAR

Work even for 1"/2.5cm. Bind off all sts as
foll: k2, *slip these 2 sts from RH needle
to LH needle, k these 2 sts tog, k1;
rep from * around. Fasten off last st.

Alligator

TAIL
With 2 strands of A held tog, cast on 3 sts.
Row 1 (WS) P3.
Row 2 (RS) Sl 1 knitwise wyib, M1, k2—4 sts.
Row 3 Sl 1 purlwise wyif, p3.
Row 4 Sl 1 knitwise wyib, M1, k3—5 sts.
Row 5 Sl 1 purlwise wyif, p4.

Gauge

21 sts and 28 rnds to 4"/10cm over St st using size 7 (4.5mm) circular needle. *Take time to check gauge.*

Row 6 Sl 1 knitwise wyib, M1, k4—6 sts. Cont to sl 1 knitwise wyib on RS rows, and sl 1 purlwise wyif on WS rows, work as foll:

BODY

Row 7 (WS) Sl 1, work (k1, p1, k1) in next st, p3tog, k1—6 sts.
Row 8 (RS) Sl 1, p5.
Row 9 Sl 1, p3tog, work (k1, p1, k1) in next st, k1—6 sts.
Row 10 Sl 1, p5.
Row 11 Rep row 7.
Row 12 Rep row 10.
Row 13 Rep row 9.
Row 14 Sl 1, M1, p5—7 sts.
Row 15 Sl 1, k1, p3tog, work (k1, p1, k1) in next st, k1.
Row 16 Sl 1, M1, p6—8 sts.
Row 17 Sl 1, k1, work (k1, p1, k1) in next st, p3tog, work (k1, p1, k1) in next st, k1—10 sts.
Row 18 Sl 1, p9.
Row 19 Sl 1, [work (k1, p1, k1) in next st, p3tog] twice, k1—10 sts.
Row 20 Sl 1, p9.
Row 21 Sl 1, [p3tog, work (k1, p1, k1) in next st] twice, k1—10 sts.
Row 22 Sl 1, M1, p9—11 sts.
Row 23 Sl 1, [work (k1, p1, k1) in next st, p3tog] twice, work (k1, p1, k1) in next st, k1—13 sts.
Row 24 Sl 1, p12—13 sts.
Row 25 Sl 1, [p3tog, work (k1, p1, k1) in next st] twice, p3tog, k1—11 sts.
Row 26 Sl 1, M1, p10—12 sts.
Row 27 Sl 1, [work (k1, p1, k1) in next st, p3tog] twice, work (k1, p1, k1) in next st, k2—14 sts.
Row 28 Sl 1, p13—14 sts.
Row 29 Sl 1, [p3tog, work (k1, p1, k1) in next st] 3 times, k1—14 sts.
Row 30 Sl 1, p13—14 sts.
Row 31 Sl 1, [work (k1, p1, k1) in next st, p3tog] 3 times, k1—14 sts.
Row 32 Rep row 30. Rep rows 29–32 until piece measures 8½"/21.5cm from beg, end with a RS row.

HEAD

Row 1 (WS) Sl 1, purl to end.
Row 2 (RS) Sl 1, knit to end.
Rep rows 1 and 2 until piece meas approx 10 ½"/26.5cm from beg, end with a WS row.

UPPER JAW

Row 1 (RS) K7, place rem 7 sts on holder for lower jaw.
Rows 2 and 4 Sl 1, p6.
Rows 3 and 5 Sl 1, k6.
Row 6 Sl 1, [p2tog, p1] twice—5 sts.
Rows 7, 9 and 11 Sl 1, k4.
Rows 8, 10 and 12 Sl 1, p4.
Row 13 Sl 1, ssk, k2tog—3 sts.
Row 14 Sl 1, p2tog—2 sts.
Row 15 Ssk. Fasten off last st.

LOWER JAW

Place 7 st from holder back to LH needle, ready for RS row.
Rows 1, 3 and 5 Sl 1, k6.
Rows 2 and 4 Sl 1, p6.
Row 6 Sl 1, [p2tog, p1] twice—5 sts.
Rows 7, 9 and 11 Sl 1, k4.
Rows 8, 10 and 12 Sl 1, p4.
Row 13 Sl 1, ssk, k2tog—3 sts.
Row 14 Sl 1, p2tog—2 sts.
Row 15 Ssk. Fasten off last st.

FRONT LEG

Position alligator body so RS is facing and lower jaw is at top. Measure and mark 3 ½"/9cm from tip of jaw. With 2 strands of B held tog, pick up and k 1 st in each of next 4 sl sts along side edge of body.
Row 1 (WS) P4.
Row 2 Sl 1, k3—4 sts.
Row 3 Sl 1, p3.
Row 4 Sl 1, M1, k1, M1, k2tog—5 sts.
Row 5 Sl 1, p4.
Row 6 Sl 1, M1, [k1, M1] twice, k2tog—7 sts. Bind off all sts purlwise.

BACK LEG

Position alligator body so RS is facing and lower jaw is at top. Measure and mark 4"/10cm from front leg. With 2 strands of B held tog, pick up and k 1 st in each of next 4 sl sts along side edge of body. Cont to work same as front leg.

Finishing

Lightly block sweater to measurements. Lightly block alligator's head and legs. Graft underarm sts tog using Kitchener stitch. Wrap and pin alligator body around left side edge of sweater so bottom of legs are ½"/1.3cm from bottom edge of sweater. Sew body in place using a single strand of A and legs using a single strand of B. Sew on button eye, or use embroidery stitches. ■

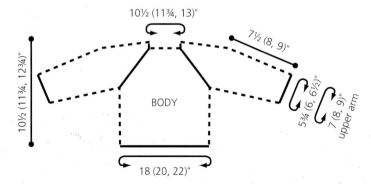

10½ (11¾, 13)"

7½ (8, 9)"

10½ (11¾, 12¾)"

BODY

5¾ (6, 6½)"

7 (8, 9)" upper arm

18 (20, 22)"

38

Mitered Edge Blanket

Squares knit in a variegated yarn form a jazzy border on a cover-up with an eye-catching shape.

DESIGNED BY AMY POLCYN

INTERMEDIATE

Knitted measurements

Approx 31" x 31"/78.5cm x 78.5cm

Materials

- 3 3½oz/100g balls (each approx 220yd/201m) of Cascade Yarns *220 Superwash* (superwash wool) in #838 rose (MC)
- 2 3½oz/100g hanks (each approx 220yd/201m) of Cascade Yarns *220 Superwash Paints* (superwash wool) in #9858 fruit smoothie (CC)
- One pair size 7 (4.5mm) needles *or size to obtain gauge*
- Size 7 (4.5mm) circular needle, 36"/91cm length
- One set (5) size 7 (4.5mm) double-pointed needles (dpns)
- Stitch marker

Notes

1) Border of blanket is made first.
2) Border is made of 4 strips that are sewn together at each corner.
3) Center of blanket is picked up along inner edge of border, then worked in the rnd to the center.

Border

SQUARES (make 16)
With straight needles and CC, cast on 20 sts, pm, cast on 21 sts——-41 sts.
Row 1 (RS) Knit.
Row 2 Knit to 1 st before marker, sl next st to RH needle, drop marker, sl st on RH needle back to LH needle, S2KP, sl this st back to LH needle, pm, sl st back to RH needle, knit to end. Rep rows 1 and 2 until 3 sts rem.
Last row K3tog. Fasten off last st.

STRIPS (make 4)
Place 2 squares RS up on work surface so cast-on edges are at bottom, last row is at top and two side corners touch.

TRIANGLES
With RS facing, straight needles and MC, pick up and k 20 sts along LH edge of right square, pick up and knit 1 st where corners touch, pm, then pick up and k 20 sts along RH edge of left square.
Row 1 (WS) Knit to 1 st before marker, sl next st to RH needle, drop marker, sl st on RH needle back to LH needle, S2KP, sl this st back to LH needle, pm, sl st back to RH needle, knit to end.
Row 2 Ssk, knit to last 2 sts, k2tog. Rep Rows 1 and 2 until 3 sts rem.

Last row K3tog. Fasten off last st. Cont to assemble strip until 4 squares are joined by 3 triangles.

JOINING STRIPS
Place strips WS up on work surface with one at top, one at bottom and one at each side forming a square border. Sew corners together.

Center square

Note Change to dpn when there are too few sts to work with circular needle.
With RS of border facing, circular needle and MC, *pick up and k 90 sts along inside edge of border, pick up and k 1 st in corner seam, pm; rep from * around 3 times more——-364 sts. Turn work so WS is facing. Join to work in the rnd.
Rnd 1 *Knit to 1 st before next marker, sl next st to RH needle, drop marker, sl st on RH needle back to LH needle, S2KP, sl this st back to LH needle, pm, sl st back to RH needle; rep from * around 3 times more——-8 sts dec. **Rnd 2** Purl. Rep rnds 1 and 2 until 12 sts rem. Cut yarn, leaving an 8"/20.5cm tail, and thread through rem sts. Pull tog tightly and secure end.

Finishing

Block piece lightly to measurements. ■

Gauge

20 sts and 40 rows to 4"/10cm over garter st (k every row) using size 7 (4.5mm) needles. *Take time to check gauge.*

Fair Isle Cardigan

Baby's first holiday needs a special sweater to match! A red and white Fair Isle pattern puts everyone in the spirit.

DESIGNED BY TANIS GRAY

Sizes
Instructions are written for size 6 months. Changes for 12 and 18–24 months are in parentheses.

Knitted measurements
Chest (closed) 22 (24, 27)"/56 (61, 68.5)cm
Length 12½ (13½, 14½)"/31.5 (34, 37)cm
Upper arm 6½ (7¾, 9)"/16.5 (19.5, 23)cm

Materials
■ 1 (2, 2) 3½oz/100g balls (each approx 220yd/201m) of Cascade Yarns *220 Superwash* (superwash wool) each in #809 really red (MC) and #910A winter white (CC)

■ Size 7 (4.5mm) circular needle, 32"/81cm length *or size to obtain gauge*

■ One set (5) size 7 (4.5mm) double-pointed needles (dpns)

■ Stitch holders

■ Stitch markers

■ Three ⅝"/16mm buttons

Notes
1) Yoke and body are worked back and forth in one piece from the neck down.
2) Sleeves are worked in the round.

Yoke
Beg at neck edge with circular needle and MC, cast on 65 (64, 65) sts. Knit next row.
Next row (WS) K 4 (4, 5) sts (button band), pm, p 57 (56, 55) sts, pm, k 4 (4, 5) sts (buttonhole band).
Inc row 1 (RS) K 4 (4, 5) sts, sl marker, k 9 (9, 8) sts (left front), yo, k1, yo, k5 sts (left sleeve), yo, k1, yo, k 25 (24, 25) sts (back), yo, k1, yo, k5 sts (right sleeve), yo, k1, yo, k 9 (9, 8) sts (right front), sl marker, k 4 (4, 5) sts—73 (72, 73) sts. Keeping 4 (4, 5) sts each side in garter st for front bands and rem sts in St st, work next row even.
Inc (and buttonhole) row 2 (RS)
K 4 (4, 5), sl marker, k 10 (10, 9), yo, k1, yo, k7, yo, k1, yo, k 27 (26, 27), yo, k1, yo, k7, yo, k1, yo, k 10 (10, 9), sl marker, k 0 (0, 1), k2tog, yo, k2—81 (80, 81) sts. Work next row even.
Inc row 3 (RS) K 4 (4, 5), sl marker, k 11 (11, 10), yo, k1, yo, k9, yo, k1, yo, k 29 (28, 29), yo, k1, yo, k9, yo, k1, yo, k 11 (11, 10), sl marker, k 4 (4, 5)—89 (88, 89) sts. Work next row even.
Inc row 4 (RS) K 4 (4, 5), sl marker, k 12 (12, 11), yo, k1, yo, k11, yo, k1, yo, k 31 (30, 31), yo, k1, yo, k11, yo, k1, yo, k 12 (12, 11), sl marker, k 4 (4, 5)—97 (96, 97) sts. Work next row even.
Inc row 5 (RS) K 4 (4, 5), sl marker, k 13 (13, 12), yo, k1, yo, k13, yo, k1, yo, k 33 (32, 33), yo, k1, yo, k13, yo, k1, yo, k 13 (13, 12), sl marker, k 4 (4, 5)—105 (104, 105) sts. Work next row even.

Gauge
19 sts and 24 rows to 4"/10cm over St st using size 7 (4.5mm) circular needle.
Take time to check gauge.

Fair Isle Cardigan

39

Inc (buttonhole) row 6 (RS) K 4 (4, 5), sl marker, k 14 (14, 13), yo, k1, yo, k15, yo, k1, yo, k 35 (34, 35), yo, k1, yo, k15, yo, k1, yo, k 14 (14, 13), sl marker, k 0 (0, 1), k2tog, yo, k2—113 (112, 113) sts. Work next row even. Cont to work incs as established, working 1 more st to each front and 2 sts to back and each sleeve every RS row 7 (10, 13) times more—169 (192, 217) sts. AT THE SAME TIME, work one more buttonhole on inc row 10.

DIVIDE FOR BODY SLEEVES
Next row (RS) K 4 (4, 5), sl marker, k 23 (26, 28) sts, place next 31 (37, 43) sts on holder (left sleeve), k 53 (58, 65) sts (back), place next 31 (37, 43) sts on holder (right sleeve), k 23 (26, 28) sts, sl marker, k 4 (4, 5)—107 (118, 131) sts.

BODY
Work even for 13 rows, end with a WS row.

BEG CHART PAT
Row 1 (RS) K 4 (4, 5) sl marker, work 11-st rep 9 (10, 11) times, sl marker, k 4 (4, 5). Cont to foll chart in this way to row 25. Cont with MC only for 3 rows, end with a WS row. Change to CC. Work in garter st (knit every row) for 6 rows. Bind off purlwise.

SLEEVES
With RS facing, dpn and MC, k 31 (37, 43) sts from sleeve holder. Divide sts evenly between 4 needles. Join and pm for beg of rnds. Work around in St st (knit every rnd) for 4¼ (4¾, 5¾)"/10.5 (12, 14.5)cm. Change to CC. Work around in garter st (knit one rnd, purl one rnd) for 6 rnds. Bind off purlwise.

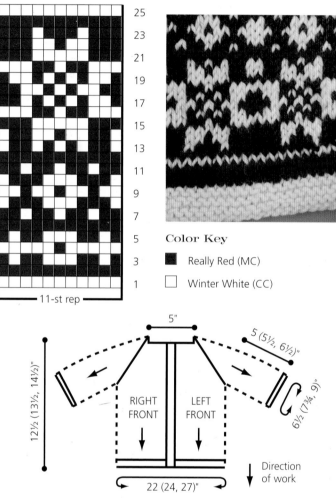

25 23 21 19 17 15 13 11 9 7 5 3 1

← 11-st rep →

Color Key
- ■ Really Red (MC)
- □ Winter White (CC)

Finishing
Block piece to measurements.

COLLAR
With WS facing, circular needle and CC, pick up and k 65 (64, 65) sts along neck edge. Work in garter st for 19 rows. Bind off purlwise. Sew on buttons. ■

5"

5 (5½, 6½)"

12½ (13½, 14½)"

RIGHT FRONT   LEFT FRONT

6½ (7¾, 9)"

22 (24, 27)"

Direction of work

Ruffled Top and Pants

Your little girl will love to tiptoe through the tulips in this darling ensemble featuring ruffles and embroidery.

DESIGNED BY CHERYL MURRAY

INTERMEDIATE

Sizes

Instructions are written for size 6 months. Changes for 12 and 18 months are in parentheses.

Knitted measurements

TOP
Chest 20 (22, 24)"/51 (56, 61)cm
Length 12 (14, 15¾)"/30.5 (35.5, 40)cm

PANTS
Hip 19½ (21¼, 22¾)"/49.5 (54, 58)cm
Length 14 (15, 16)"/35.5 (38, 40.5)cm

Materials

■ 2 (2, 3) 3½oz/100g balls (each approx 220yd/200m) of Cascade Yarns *220 Superwash* (superwash wool) in #1940 peach (MC)

■ 1 (2, 2) balls in #820 lemon (CC)

■ Size 7 (4.5mm) 32"/80cm circular needle *or size needed to obtain gauge*

■ Size 7 (4.5mm) 24"/60cm circular needle

■ Size 6 (4mm) 24"/60cm circular needle

■ One set (5) size 7 (4.5mm) double-pointed needles (dpns)

■ Stitch holders

■ ½ yd/.5m of ½"/1.3cm elastic (approx 1–2"/2.5–5cm smaller than desired waist size)

■ One ⅜"/1cm button (LaMode #41321)

■ Waste yarn

■ Tapestry needle

Short Row Wrap and Turn (w&t) on RS row (on WS row)

1) Wyib (wyif), sl next st purlwise.
2) Move yarn between the needles to the front (back).
3) Sl the same st back to LH needle. Turn work. One st is wrapped.
4) When working the wrapped st, insert RH needle under the wrap and work it tog with the corresponding st on needle.

Top

RUFFLE

With 32"/80cm circular and MC, cast on 250 (280, 300) sts. Pm and join, being careful not to twist cast-on.
Rnd 1 Purl.
Rnd 2 *K2tog, yo; rep from * to end.
Rnds 3–6 Knit.
Rnd 7 *K2tog; rep from * to end—125 (140, 150) sts.
Leave sts on needle.

SKIRT

With larger 24"/60cm circular and CC, cast on 125 (140, 150) sts. Pm and join, being careful not to twist cast-on. Place ruffle behind cast-on and *knit 1 st from cast-on together with 1 st from ruffle; rep from * to end. Work even in St st (k on RS, p on WS) for 6 (7½, 8½)"/15 (19, 21.5)cm.
Next rnd *K3, k2tog; rep from * to end—100 (112, 120) sts.
Place all sts on holder.

BODICE

With larger 24"/60cm circular and MC, cast on 100 (112, 120) sts. Pm and join, being careful not to twist cast-on. Place skirt behind cast-on and *knit 1 st from cast-on together with 1 st from skirt; rep from * to end. Place a 2nd side

Gauge

20 sts and 28 rows to 4"/10cm over St st using larger circular needle. *Take time to check gauge.*

117

Ruffled Top and Pants

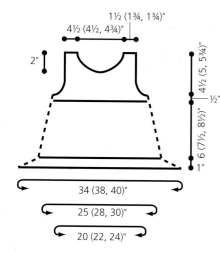

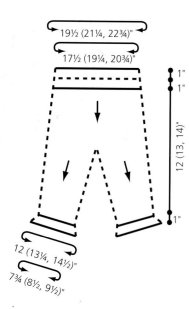

marker between sts 50 and 51 (56 and 57, 60 and 61).
Work 3 rnds even in St st.

DIVIDE FOR FRONT AND BACK
Bind off 3 (4, 5) sts, k to marker. Place rem 50 (56, 60) sts on holder for back.
FRONT
Bind off 3 (4, 5) sts, p to end of row.

ARMHOLE SHAPING
Dec row (RS) K1, ssk, k to last 3 sts, k2tog, k1.
Rep dec row every RS row 3 times more—36 (40, 42) sts.
Work even in St st until bodice measures 2½ (3,3¾)"/6.5 (7.5, 9.5)cm, ending with a WS row.

NECK AND SHOULDER SHAPING
K14 (16, 16), join a 2nd ball of yarn and bind off next 8 (8, 10) sts, k to end—14 (16, 16) sts each side.

RIGHT SIDE
Row 1 (WS) Purl.
Row 2 Bind off 2 sts, k to end—12 (14, 14) sts.
Rows 3 and 5 P to last 3 sts, p2tog tbl, p1.
Row 4 and 6 K1, ssk, k to end.
Row 7 Rep row 3—7 (9, 9) sts.
Work even in St st until bodice measures 4½ (5, 5¾)"/11.5 (12.5, 14.5)cm, ending with a RS row.
Bind off 3 (4, 4) sts, p to end; k 1 row.
Bind off rem 4 (5, 5) sts.

LEFT SIDE
Row 1 (WS) Bind off 2 sts, p to end—12 (14, 14) sts.
Rows 2 and 4 K to last 3 sts, k2tog.
Rows 3 and 5 P1, p2tog, p to end.

Row 6 Rep row 2—7 (9, 9) sts.
Work even in St st until bodice measures 4½ (5, 5¾)"/11.5 (12.5, 14.5)cm, ending with a WS row.
Bind off 3 (4, 4) sts, k to end; p 1 row.
Bind off rem 4 (5, 5) sts.

BACK
Place back sts from holder onto needle with RS facing and join MC. Cont in St st, bind off 3 (4, 5) sts at beg of next 2 rows.

ARMHOLE SHAPING
Dec row (RS) K1, ssk, k to last 3 sts, k2tog, k1.
Rep dec row every RS row 3 times more—36 (40, 42) sts.
Work in St st until bodice measures 2¼ (2¾, 3½)"/5.5 (7, 9)cm, end with a RS row.

KEYHOLE SHAPING
Row 1 (WS) P16 (18, 19), k4, p16 (18, 19).
Row 2 K18 (20, 21), attach a 2nd ball of yarn and k18 (20, 21).
Rows 3–11 Work both sides at once in St st, keeping 2 sts at each neck edge in garter st (k every row).
Row 12 (buttonhole row) K to last 2 sts of right side, k2; for left side, k1, yo, k2tog, k to end.
Row 13 Purl.

NECK SHAPING
Bind off 10 (10, 11), sts at each neck edge once, then dec 1 st at each neck edge once—7 (9, 9) sts each side.
Bind off 3 (4, 4) sts at each armhole edge once, then bind off rem 4 (5, 5) sts at each armhole edge.

Ruffled Top and Pants

Finishing
Sew shoulder seams.

NECKBAND
With RS facing, larger needle and MC, be at center back, pick up and k67 (67, 71) sts evenly around neck opening. K 1 row. P 1 row. Bind off loosely knitwise.

ARMBANDS
With RS facing, MC and dpns, starting at underarm, pick up and k47 (53, 61) sts evenly around armhole. Pm and join. P 2 rnds. Bind off loosely purlwise. Sew button opposite buttonhole.

FLOWER PETALS (make 5)
With larger needles and MC, cast on 1 st.
Row 1 (RS) K in (front, back, front, back, front) of same st—5 sts.
Rows 2, 4, 6 and 8 Purl.
Rows 3, 5 and 7 Knit.
Row 9 Ssk, k1, k2tog—3 sts.
Row 10 Sl 1, p2tog, psso—1 st.
Fasten off.
Run a length of yarn through the cast-on edge of all petals. Pull tightly to gather into a circle and secure. Attach flower to skirt with whipstitch around all petals, stuffing ends inside petals for added dimension.
With CC, make 5 French knots in center of flower.
With MC, use running st to create random swirl patterns around flower.

Pants
Note Pants are worked from the waist-band down to the cuffs.
With CC and smaller 24"/60cm circular needle, cast on 88 (96, 104) sts. Pm and join, being careful not to twist cast-on. Place a 2nd side marker between sts 44 and 45 (48 and 49, 52 and 53).

Work 7 rnds in St st (k every rnd). Change to larger needle.
Turning rnd *P2tog, yo; rep from * to end. Work 7 rnds in St st. Change to MC and work 8 rnds in St st.
Inc rnd M1 (see page 4), k to marker, M1, k to end. Rep inc rnd every 8th (9th, 10th) rnd 4 times more—98 (106, 114) sts.
AT THE SAME TIME, when piece measures 1, 3 and 5"/2.5, 7.5 and 12.5cm from color change, insert short rows on back side only as follows:
Short row 1 K to 5 sts before side marker, w&t, p to 5 sts before end of rnd marker, w&t.
Short row 2 K to 10 sts before side marker, w&t, p to 10 sts before end of rnd marker, w&t.
Cont working in St st, lifting and working wraps together with the wrapped st.

After last side inc, k 1 rnd. Mark center front and center back sts.
Inc rnd *K to next center marked st, M1, k1, M1; rep from * once, k to end. Rep inc rnd every rnd twice more—110 (118, 126) sts.

DIVIDE FOR LEGS
Slip first and last 24 (26, 28) sts onto waste yarn; place next 7 sts onto a dpn; slip next 48 (52, 56) sts onto a 2nd length of waste yarn; place rem 7 sts onto a 2nd dpn—48 (52, 56) sts held for each leg. Graft sts on dpns together to form crotch.

SHAPE LEGS
Transfer sts for one leg to dpns. Pick up and k5 sts along side of crotch and join—53 (57, 61) sts. Mark center picked-up st for inseam and end of rnd. Work even in St st for 2 (2, 3)"/5 (5, 7.5)cm.
Dec rnd K2tog, k to 3 sts before end of rnd, ssk, k1.
Rep dec rnd every 4th rnd 6 times more—39 (43, 47) sts.
Work even in St st until pants measure 13 (14, 15)"/33 (35.5, 38)cm from turning rnd.
Next rnd *P2tog; rep from * to last st, p1—20 (22, 24) sts.
Change to CC.
Next rnd *K in (front, back, front) of next st; rep from * to end—60 (66, 72) sts. Work 4 rnds even in St st.
Next rnd *K2tog, yo; rep from * to end. K 1 rnd. Bind off loosely purlwise. Repeat for 2nd leg.

Finishing
Fold cast-on edge to inside to form casing and sew in place, leaving an opening. Weave elastic through casing, adjust waist width and casing opneing closed. ■

Striped Cardi

A light outer layer when the weather is getting warmer, this cheery number is a welcome breath of spring.

DESIGNED BY DEBBIE O'NEILL

INTERMEDIATE

Sizes
Instructions are written for size 3 months. Changes for 6 and 12 months are in parentheses.

Knitted measurements
Chest (closed) 19 (21, 22½)"/48 (53.5, 57)cm
Length 10¾ (11¾, 12¾)"/27.5 (30, 32.5)cm
Upper arm 6½ (7¼, 8)"/16.5 (18.5, 20.5)cm

Materials
▪ 1 (2, 2) 3½oz/100g balls (each approx 220yd/201m) of Cascade Yarns *220 Superwash* (superwash wool) each in #824 yellow (A) and #871 white (B)
▪ Size 6 (4mm) circular needle, 24"/61cm length *or size to obtain gauge*
▪ One set (5) size 6 (4mm) double-pointed needles (dpns)
▪ Stitch holders
▪ Stitch markers
▪ Three ⁵⁄₈"/16mm buttons

Notes
1) Yoke and body are worked back and forth in one piece from the neck down.
2) Sleeves are worked in the round.

Stitch glossary
M1R (make 1 right) Insert left needle from back to front into the horizontal strand between the last st worked and the next st on left needle. Knit this strand through the front loop to twist the st.
M1L (make 1 left) Insert left needle from front to back into the horizontal strand between the last st worked and the next st on left needle. Knit this strand through the back loop to twist the st.
Inc Knit in front and back of st.

Stripe pattern
Working in St st, *work 6 rows A, 4 rows B; rep from * (10 rows) for stripe pat.

Cardigan
YOKE
Beg at neck edge, with circular needle and A, cast on 66 sts. Knit next row.
Next row (WS) P12, pm, p1, pm, p7, pm, p1, pm, p24, pm, p1, pm, p7, pm, p1, pm, p12. Cont in St st (knit on RS, purl on WS) and stripe pattern as foll:
Inc row (RS) *Knit to marker, M1R, sl marker, k1, sl marker, M1L; rep from * 3 times more. Purl next row. Rep last 2 rows 11 (13, 15) times more—162 (178, 194) sts.

DIVIDE FOR BODY SLEEVES
Next row (RS) K 24 (26, 28) sts (left front), place next 33 (37, 41) sts on holder (left sleeve), cast on 3 sts (left underarm), k 48 (52, 56) sts (back), place next 33 (37, 41) sts on holder (right sleeve), cast on 3 sts (right underarm), k 24 (26, 28) sts (right front)—102 (110, 118) sts.

Gauge
22 sts and 32 rows to 4"/10cm over St st using size 6 (4mm) circular needle. *Take time to check gauge.*

Striped Cardi

41

BODY
Cont in stripe pat as established until piece meaasures 6½ (7, 7½)"/16.5 (18, 19)cm from underarm cast-on. Bind off.

SLEEVES
With RS facing, dpn and color for stripe in progress, skip first st of underarm cast-on sts, pick up and k 1 st in each of next 2 sts, k 33 (37, 41) sts from sleeve holder, pick up and k 1 st rem st of underarm cast-on—36 (40, 44) sts. Divide sts evenly between 4 needles. Join and pm for beg of rnds. Work around in St st (knit every rnd) and stripe pat for 1"/2.5cm.
Dec rnd K1, k2tog, knit to last 2 sts, ssk. Rep dec rnd every 12th (12th, 10th) rnd 3 (3, 4) times more—28 (32,34) sts. Work even until piece measures 6½ (7, 7½)"/16.5 (18, 19)cm from underarm cast-on. Bind off.

Finishing
Block piece to measurements.

OUTER BAND
With RS facing, circular needle and B, pick up and k 56 (60, 66) sts evenly spaced along right front edge, 64 sts along neck edge, then 56 (60, 66) sts along left front edge—176 (184, 196) sts. **Next (inc) row (WS)** *Knit to corner st, work inc; rep from * once more—178 (186, 198) sts.
Knit next 2 rows.
Next (buttonhole) row (RS) K 36 (37, 40), *k2tog, yo twice, k2tog, k 4 (5, 6); rep from * twice more, knit to end.
Next row Knit, working (k1, p1) in each double yo.
Next (inc) row (RS) *Knit to corner st, work inc; rep from * once more—180 (188, 200) sts. Bind off loosely purlwise. Sew on buttons. ■

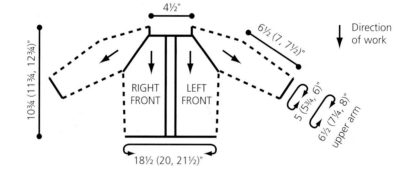

122

Tennis Vest

It will be "love all" around when you knit this jaunty topper with an ace cable motif.

DESIGNED BY HEIDI KOZAR

■■■■
EXPERIENCED

Sizes

Instructions are written for size 6 months. Changes for 12 and 18 months are in parentheses.

Knitted measurements

Chest 20 (22, 24)"/51 (56, 61)cm
Length 11½ (13, 14½)"/29 (33, 37)cm

Materials

■ 1 (2, 2) 3½oz/100g balls (each approx 220yd/200m) of Cascade Yarns *220 Superwash* (superwash wool) in #816 gray (MC)

■ 1 ball each in #820 lemon (A) and #892 spaceneedle (B)

■ One pair each sizes 6 and 7 (4 and 4.5mm) needles *or size to obtain gauge*

■ Size 6 (4mm) circular needle, 12"/30cm long

■ Cable needle (cn)

■ Safety pin

■ Stitch markers

Stitch glossary

3-st RPC Sl 1 st to cn and hold to *back*, k2, p1 from cn.

3-st LPC Sl 2 sts to cn and hold to *front*, p1, k2 from cn.

4-st RC Sl 2 sts to cn and hold to *back*, k2, k2 from cn.

4-st LC Sl 2 sts to cn and hold to *front*, k2, k2 from cn.

5-st RPC Sl 3 sts to cn and hold to *back*, k2, then sl purl st from cn back to LH needle and purl it, then k2 from cn.

5-st LPC Sl 3 sts to cn and hold to *front*, k2, then sl purl st from cn back to LH needle and purl it, then k2 from cn.

M1R (make 1 right) Insert LH needle from *back* to *front* into the strand between last st worked and the next st on the LH needle. Knit into the front loop to twist the st.

M1L (make 1 left) Insert LH needle from *front to back* into the strand between last st worked and the next st on the LH needle. Knit into the back loop to twist the st.

Front

With larger needles and A, cast on 54 (54, 62) sts.
Beg with a knit row, work in St st (k on RS, p on WS) for 4 rows. **Change to smaller needles and B.
Next row (RS) Knit. Beg with row 2, cont in k2, p2 rib for 5 rows, end with a WS row. Change to A.
Next row (RS) Knit. Work row 2 of k2, p2 rib. Change to B.

Next row (RS) Knit. Beg with row 2, cont in k2, p2 rib for 5 rows, end with a WS row. Change to larger needles and MC.**
Place a marker each side of center 18 sts.
Next (inc/dec) row (RS) Knit to first marker inc 2 (4, 3) sts evenly spaced, sl marker, [p2, k2] twice, p2tog, [k2, p2] twice, sl marker, knit to end inc 2 (4, 3) sts evenly spaced—57 (61, 67) sts.

BEG CHART PAT
Row 1 (WS) Purl to marker, sl marker, work 17 sts of chart, sl marker, purl to end. Cont to foll chart in this way to row 16, then rep rows 1–16 once (once, twice) more, then rows 1–7 (1–15, 1–7) once more. Piece measures approx 7½ (8½, 9½)"/19 (21.5, 24)cm from beg.

ARMHOLE AND NECK SHAPING
Row 1 (RS) Knit to first marker, sl marker, p3, [k4, p3] twice, sl marker, knit to end.
Row 2 (inc) 2 Purl to first marker, sl marker, k3, p4, k1, M1R, k1, M1L, k1, p4, k3, sl marker, purl to end—59 (63, 69) sts.
Row 3 Bind off 3 (3, 4) sts, knit to 3 sts before first marker, k2tog, k1, sl marker, p2tog tbl, p1, 4-st RC, p2, place center st on safety pin, join a 2nd ball of MC, p2, 4-st LC, p1, p2tog, sl marker, k1, ssk, knit to end. Cont to work both sides at once, as foll:

Gauge

20 sts and 30 rows to 4"/10cm over St st (k on RS, p on WS) using larger needles. *Take time to check gauge.*

Tennis Vest

Row 4 With first ball of yarn, bind off 3 (3, 4) sts, purl to first marker, k2, p4, k2; with 2nd ball of yarn, k2, p4, k2, sl marker, purl to end.

Row 5 With first ball of yarn, k1, ssk, knit to first marker, sl marker, p2, k4, p2; with 2nd ball of yarn, p2, k4, p2, sl marker, knit to last 3 sts, k2tog, k1.

Row 6 K the knit sts and p the purl sts.

Row 7 With first ball of yarn, k1, ssk, knit to 3 sts before first marker, k2tog, k1, sl marker, p2tog tbl, 4-st RC, p2; with 2nd ball of yarn, p2, 4-st LC, p2tog, sl marker, k1, ssk, knit to last 3 sts, ktog, k1.

Row 8 Rep row 6.

Row 9 With first ball of yarn, k1, ssk, knit to first marker, sl marker, p1, k4, p2; with 2nd ball of yarn, p2, k4, p1, sl marker, knit to last 3 sts, k2tog, k1.

Row 10 Rep row 6—19 (21, 23) sts each side. Armhole shaping is now complete. Cont to work 4-st RC and 4-st LC on next row, then every 4th row to end of piece, AT THE SAME TIME, cont to dec 1 st from each neck edge on next row (outside of cable panels), then every 4th row 2 (3, 4) times more, then every other row 4 times—12 (13, 14) sts each side. Work even until armhole measures 4 (4½, 5)"/10 (11.5, 12.5)cm, end with a WS row. Bind off sts each side, working k2tog

twice over cable sts while binding off.

Back
With larger needles and A, cast on 50 (54, 58) sts. Work in St st for 4 rows. Rep from ** to ** same as front.

Next (inc) row (RS) Knit, inc 2 (2, 4) sts evenly spaced—52 (56, 62) sts. Beg with a purl row, cont in St st and work even until piece measures same length as front to underarm, end with a WS row.

ARMHOLE SHAPING
Bind off 3 (3, 4) sts at beg of next 2 rows.

Next (dec) row (RS) K1, ssk, knit to last 3 sts, k2tog, k1. Purl next row. Rep last 2 rows twice more—40 (44, 48) sts. Work even until piece measures same length as front to shoulder, end with a WS row. Bind off.

Finishing
Lightly block pieces to measurements. Sew shoulder seams.

NECKBAND
With RS facing, circular needle and B, beg at left shoulder seam and pick up and k 18 (20, 22) sts evenly spaced along left neck edge to center st, k1 from safety pin, then mark this st with safety pin, pick up and k 18 (20, 22) sts evenly spaced along right

neck edge to right shoulder seam, then pick up and k 22 (24, 26) sts evenly spaced along back neck edge—59 (65, 71) sts. Join and pm for beg of rnds.

Rnd 1 Work in k1, p1 rib to center marked sf, k1 for center st, beg with a p1, work in rib to end of rnd. Change to A.

Rnd 2 Knit to 1 st before center st, S2KP, knit to end of rnd.

Rnd 3 Cont in rib as established, and k center st. Change to B.

Rnd 4 Rep rnd 2.

Rnd 5 Rep rnd 3.

Rnd 6 Work in rib to 1 st before center st, S2KP, work in rib to end.

Rnd 7 Work in rib and k center st.
Bind off sts loosely in rib.

ARMBANDS
With RS facing, smaller needles and B, pick up and k 49 (55, 61) sts evenly along each armhole edge.

Row 1 (WS) P1, *k1, p1; rep from * to end. Change to A.

Row 2 Knit.

Row 3 Rep row 1. Change to B.

Row 4 Knit.

Row 5 Rep row 1.

Row 6 K1, *p1, k1; rep from * to end. Bind off loosely in rib. Sew side and armband seams. ∎

Stitch Key

☐	K on RS, p on WS
⊟	P on RS, k on WS
	3-st RPC
	3-st LPC
	4-st RC
	4-st LC
	5-st RPC
	5-st LPC

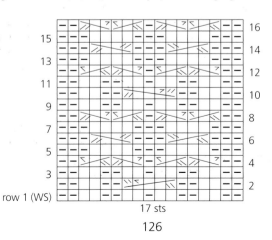

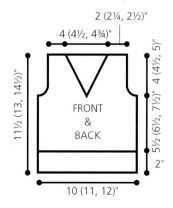

Cabled Tunic

With its decorative bodice and ruffled skirt, this pretty dress will delight any little ballerina.

DESIGNED BY LEE GANT

INTERMEDIATE

Sizes
Instructions are written for size 6 months. Changes for 12 and 18 months are in parentheses.

Knitted measurements
Chest 18 (20, 22)"/45.5 (51, 56)cm
Length 14 (15, 16)"/35.5 (38, 40.5)cm

Materials
■ 2 (3, 3) 3½oz/100g balls (each approx 220yd/201m) of Cascade Yarns *220 Superwash Paints* (superwash wool) in #9860 jelly bean

■ One pair each size 5 and 7 (3.75 and 4.5mm) needles *or size to obtain gauge*

■ Two spare size 5 (3.75mm) needles

■ Size 5 (3.75mm) circular needle, 16"/40cm length

■ Cable needle (cn)

■ Stitch marker

Stitch glossary
4-st LC Sl next 2 sts to cn and hold to front, k2, k2 from cn.

Back
RUFFLES (make 3)
With smaller needles, cast on 101 (113, 125) sts. Knit next 4 rows. Cont in St st (knit on RS, purl on WS) and work even until piece measures 3"/7.5cm from beg, end with a WS row.
Dec row (RS) K1, *k3tog, k1; rep from *

to end—51 (57, 63) sts. Purl next row. Leave sts on needle. Make a 2nd ruffle to measure 2"/5cm long, end with a WS row. Rep dec row—51 (57, 63) sts. Purl next row. Join first and 2nd ruffles as foll:
Joining row (RS) With both RS facing, place shorter ruffle on top of longer ruffle so needles are parallel. Insert 3rd needle knitwise into first st of each needle and wrap yarn around each needle as if to knit, then knit these 2 sts tog and sl them off the needles. *K the next 2 sts tog in the same manner; rep from * to end. Purl next row.
Make a 3rd ruffle to measure 1"/2.5cm long, end with a WS row.
Rep dec row—51 (57, 63) sts. Purl next row. Join this ruffle to the other two in the same manner, then purl the next row, dec 1 st in center—50 (56, 62) sts.

BODY
Change to larger needles.
Cont in cable pat as foll:
Rows 1 (RS) K 3 (6, 5), *p4, k4; rep from *, end p4, k 3 (6, 5).
Row 2 and all WS rows P 3 (6, 5), *k4, p4; rep from *, end k4, p 3 (6, 5).
Row 3 K 3 (6, 5), *p4, 4-st LC;

Gauges
24 sts and 29 rows to 4"/10cm over St st using smaller needles.
21 sts and 26 rows to 4"/10cm over cable pat using larger needles.
20 sts and 26 rows to 4"/10cm over St st using larger needles.
Take time to check gauges.

Cabled Tunic

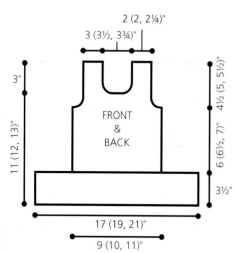

FRONT & BACK

2 (2, 2¼)"

3 (3½, 3¾)"

3"

11 (12, 13)"

4½ (5, 5½)"

6 (6½, 7)"

3½"

17 (19, 21)"

9 (10, 11)"

Quick Tip
If this is your first foray into knitting cables,
practice first on a swatch to get the hang of it.

rep from *, end p4, k 3 (6, 5).
Row 5 Rep row 1.
Row 6 Rep row 2. Rep rows 1–6 for
cable pat and work even until piece
measures 9½ (10, 10½)"/24 (25.5,
26.5)cm from beg, end with a WS row.

ARMHOLE SHAPING
Bind off 3 (4, 5) sts at beg of next 2 rows.
Dec row (RS) K1, ssk, work to last 3 sts,
k2tog, k1. Work next row even. Rep last
2 rows 1 (2, 2) times more—40 (42, 46)
sts. Discontinue cable twists on first and
last cables. Work even until armhole
measures 1½ (2, 2½)"/4 (5, 6.5)cm, end
with a WS row.

NECK SHAPING
Next row (RS) Work across first 14 (14,
15) sts, join a 2nd ball of yarn and bind
off center 12 (14, 16) sts, work to end.
Working both sides at once, work next
row even.
Dec row (RS) With first ball of yarn,
work to last 3 sts, k2tog, k1; with 2nd
ball of yarn, k1, ssk, work to end. Work
next row even. Rep last 2 rows once
more—12 (12, 13) sts. Work even until
armhole measures 4½ (5, 5½)"/11.5
(12.5, 14)cm, end with a WS row. Bind
off each side for shoulders.

Front
Work same as back.

Finishing
Block pieces to measurements. Sew
shoulder seams.

NECKBAND
With RS facing and circular needle, beg
at left shoulder seam and pick up and k
16 sts evenly spaced along left front
neck edge, 12 (14, 16) sts along front
neck edge, 16 sts along right front neck
edge to right shoulder seam, 16 sts
along right back neck edge, 12 (14, 16)
along back neck edge, 16 sts along left
back neck edge to left shoulder seam—
88 (92, 96) sts. Join and pm for beg of
rnds. Purl one rnd, knit one rnd, purl one
rnd. Bind off all sts loosely knitwise.

ARMBANDS
With RS facing and smaller needles,
pick up and k 60 (68, 76) sts evenly
spaced along armhole edge. Knit next 3
rows. Bind off all sts knitwise.
Sew side seams from armbands to ruffles.
Sew side seams of each ruffle. ■

Lace Braids Blanket

Wide, chunky twists stripe the body of this sophisticated throw.

DESIGNED BY AMY POLCYN

Knitted measurements
Approx 28" x 34½"/71cm x 87.5cm

Materials
■ 5 3½oz/100g balls (each approx 220yd/201m) of Cascade Yarns *220 Superwash* (superwash wool) in #1942 mint
■ Size 7 (4.5mm) circular needle, 36"/91cm length *or size to obtain gauge*
■ Stitch markers

Blanket
Cast on 128 sts. Purl every row until 1¾"/4.5cm from cast-on row.

BEG CHART PAT
Row 1 (WS) P3, pm, purl to last 3 sts, pm, p3.
Row 2 P3, sl marker (sm), work sts 1 and 2 of chart, then work 15-st rep 8 times, sm, p3.
Row 3 P3, sl marker (sm), work 15-st rep 8 times, then work sts 2 and 1 of chart, sm, p3. Purl first 3 sts and last 3 sts of every row, and cont to follow chart through row 12, then rep rows 1–12 for lace braids pat st.
Work even until piece measures 32¼"/ 83cm from beg, end with a WS row, leave markers on this row. Purl every row until 1¾"/4.5cm from markers. Remove markers, bind off purlwise.

Finishing
Block piece lightly to measurements.

BORDER
With RS facing, pick up and knit 171 sts along left side edge. Knit every row until 1¾"/4.5cm from picked-up row, bind off. Rep along right side edge. ■

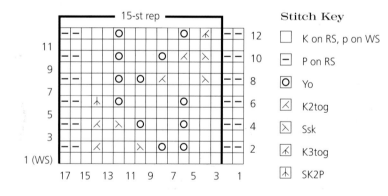

Stitch Key

□	K on RS, p on WS
−	P on RS
O	Yo
⟋	K2tog
⟍	Ssk
⋀	K3tog
⋏	SK2P

Gauge
20 sts and 28 rows to 4"/10cm over leaf pat st using size 7 (4.5mm) circular needle. *Take time to check gauge.*

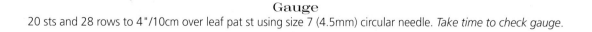

Rolled Edge Cap

This simple hat lets the colors of the variegated yarn—and baby's darling face—shine!

DESIGNED BY ANGELA JUERGENS

EASY

Sizes

Instructions are written for size newborn–3 months. Changes for size 6–12 months are in parentheses.

Knitted measurements

Head circumference
14 (16)"/35.5 (40.5)cm
Depth
5½ (6)"/14 (15)cm (excluding tab)

Materials

■ 1 3½oz/100g ball (approx 220yd/200m) of Cascade Yarns *220 Superwash Paints* (superwash wool) in #9859 tropical punch

■ One set (5) size 7 (4.5mm) double-pointed needles (dpns)
or size to obtain gauge

■ Stitch marker

Hat

Cast on 77 (88) sts, dividing sts evenly over 4 needles. Join and pm, taking care not to twist sts on needles. Work around in St st (knit every rnd) for 4½ (5)"/11.5 (12.5)cm.

CROWN SHAPING

Dec rnd 1 *K9, k2tog; rep from * around—70 (80) sts. Knit next 2 rnds.
Dec rnd 2 *K8, k2tog; rep from * around—63 (72) sts. Knit next 2 rnds.

Dec rnd 3 *K7, k2tog; rep from * around—56 (64) sts. Knit next rnd.
Dec rnd 4 *K6, k2tog; rep from * around—49 (56) sts. Knit next rnd.
Dec rnd 5 *K5, k2tog; rep from * around—42 (48) sts. Knit next rnd.
Dec rnd 6 *K4, k2tog; rep from * around—35 (40) sts. Knit next rnd.
Dec rnd 7 *K3, k2tog; rep from * around—28 (32) sts. Knit next rnd.
Dec rnd 8 *K2, k2tog; rep from * around—21 (24) sts.
Dec rnd 9 *K1, k2tog; rep from * around—14 (16) sts.
Dec rnd 10 [K2tog] 7 (8) times—7 (8) sts.

TAB

Cont in St st for 8 rnds. Cut yarn, leaving an 8"/20.5cm tail and thread through rem sts. Pull tog tightly and secure end. ■

Gauge

22 sts and 28 rnds to 4"/10cm over St st using size 7 (4.5mm) dpns.
Take time to check gauge.

Hooded Pullover

This hoodie is so comfy, rough-and-tumble tykes won't want to wear anything else.

DESIGNED BY LORNA MISER

INTERMEDIATE

Sizes

Instructions are written for size 6 months. Changes for 12 and 18 months are in parentheses.

Knitted measurements

Chest 20 (22, 24)"/51 (56, 61)cm
Length 12 (13, 14)"/30.5 (33, 35.5)cm
Upper arm 9 (10, 11)"/23 (25.5, 28)cm

Materials

- 2 (3, 3) 3½oz/100g balls (each approx 220yd/201m) of Cascade Yarns *220 Superwash Paints* (superwash wool) in #9885 clover
- Size 6 (4mm) circular needles, 16"/41cm and 24"/61cm length *or size to obtain gauge*
- One set (5) size 6 (4mm) double-pointed needles (dpns)
- Stitch holders
- Stitch markers
- One 9/16"/14mm button

Notes

1) Pullover is made in one piece from the neck down.
2) Beg of yoke is worked back and forth and the remainder of yoke and body are worked in the round.
3) Sleeves are worked in the round.

Stitch glossary

Inc Knit in front and back of st.

Pullover

Beg at neck edge, with shorter circular needle, cast on 40 sts. Do not join. Knit next row.
Next row (WS) P2, pm, p10, pm, p16, pm, p10, pm, k2.
Inc row 1 (RS) Inc, *inc in st before and in st after next marker; rep from * 3 times more, inc—50 sts. Purl next row.

Inc row 2 (RS) Inc, knit to 1 st before next marker, *inc in st before and in st after next marker; rep from * 3 times more, knit to last st, inc. Purl next row. Rep last 2 rows once more, then inc row 2 only once—80 sts.
Next row (WS) Cast on 4 sts, k4 these 4 sts (front band), pm, purl to end, pm, cast on 4 sts (front band)—88 sts.
Inc row 3 (RS) K4, sl marker, knit to 1 st before next marker, *inc in st before and in st after next marker; rep from * 3 times more, knit to last marker, sl marker, k4.
Next row K4, sl marker, purl to last marker, k4. Rep last 2 rows 4 times more—128 sts.
Inc row 4 (RS) K4, drop marker, knit to 1 st before next marker, *inc in st before and in st after next marker; rep from * 3 times more, knit to last marker, drop marker, place last 4 sts on dpn—136 sts.

YOKE JOINING

Next rnd Hold sts on dpn behind first 4 sts on LH needle so both tips point right. Insert 3rd needle knitwise into first st of each needle and k2tog, then cont in this way 3 times more, then knit to end of rnd—132 sts. Change to longer circular needle.

Gauge

21 sts and 26 rnds to 4"/10cm over St st using size 6 (4mm) circular needle.
Take time to check gauge.

Hooded Pullover

46

Inc row 5 (RS) Knit to 1 st before next marker, *inc in st before and in st after next marker; rep from * 3 times more, knit to end. Knit next rnd. Rep last 2 rnds 3 (6, 9) times more—164 (188, 212) sts.

DIVIDE FOR BODY AND SLEEVES
Dropping all markers, work as foll:
Next rnd Knit to first marker, place next 38 (44, 50) sts on holder for left sleeve, cast on 8 sts for left underarm, k 44 (50, 56) sts for back, place next 38 (44, 50) sts on holder for right sleeve, cast on 8 sts for right underarm, k 44 (50, 56) sts for front—104 (116, 128) sts.
Pm for beg of rnds.

BODY
Work around in St st (knit every rnd) until piece measures 6 (6½, 7)"/15 (16.5, 18)cm from underarm cast-on. Work around in k1, p1 rib for 1"/2.5cm. Bind off in rib.

SLEEVES
With RS facing and dpn, skip first 4 sts of underarm cast-on sts, pick up and k 1 st in each of next 4 sts, k 38 (44, 50) sts

from sleeve holder, pick up and k 1 st in each rem 4 sts of cast-on—46 (52, 58) sts. Divide sts evenly between 4 needles. Join and pm for beg of rnds. Work around in St st for 1"/2.5cm.
Dec rnd K2tog, knit to last 2 sts, ssk. Rep dec rnd every 6th rnd 4 (1, 0) times more, then every 4th rnd 0 (6, 9) times—36 (36, 38) sts. Work even until sleeve

measures 5 (5½, 6½)"/12.5 (14, 16.5)cm from beg. Work around in k1, p1 rib for 1"/2.5cm. Bind off in rib.

Finishing
Block piece to measurements.

HOOD
With longer circular needle, pick up and k 56 sts along entire neck edge.
Next row (WS) K4, p24, pm, p24, k4.
Next (inc and buttonhole) row (RS) Knit to 1 st before marker, inc, sl marker, inc, knit to last 3 sts, yo, k2tog, k1—58 sts.
Next row (WS) K4, purl to last 4 sts, k4.
Next (inc) row (RS) Knit to 1 st before marker, inc, sl marker, inc, knit to end.
Next row (WS) K4, purl to last 4 sts, k4. Rep last 2 rows 2 (3, 4) times more—64 (66, 68) sts. Work even until piece measures 7"/18cm, end with a WS row.
Next (dec) row (RS) Knit to 2 sts before marker, ssk, sl marker, k2tog, knit to end.
Next row (WS) K4, purl to last 4 sts, k4. Rep last 2 rows 4 (5, 6) times more— 54 sts. Bind off and sew hood seam, or join using 3-needle bind-off.
Sew on button. ■

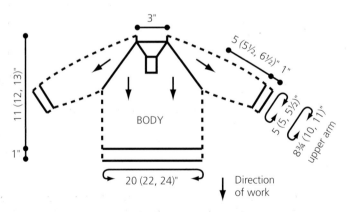

Fisherman's Pullover

Multiple cables, a classic color and a shawl collar add up to a timeless design that's perfect for a little landlubber.

DESIGNED BY LEE GANT

Sizes
Instructions are written for size 6–9 months. Changes for 12–18 months are in parentheses.

Knitted measurements
Chest 22 (26)"/56 (66)cm
Length 12 (14)"/30.5 (35.5)cm
Upper arm 8 (10)"/20.5 (25.5)cm

Materials
■ 3 (4) 3½oz/100g balls (each approx 220yd/201m) of Cascade Yarns *220 Superwash* (superwash wool) in #892 spaceneedle
■ One pair each sizes 4 and 6 (3.5 and 4mm) needles *or size to obtain gauge*
■ Size 4 (3.5mm) circular needle, 29"/73cm length
■ Cable needle (cn)
■ Stitch holder
■ Stitch markers

Notes
1) The difference between the seed st row gauge and the cable pats row gauge (same as St st) creates an automatic slope to the shoulders.
2) Always measure for length down center cable and not seed st sections unless stated otherwise.

Stitch glossary
6-st RC Sl next 3 sts to cn and hold to *back*, k3, k3 from cn.
6-st LC Sl next 3 sts to cn and hold to *front*, k3, k3 from cn.

K2, p2 rib
(over a multiple of 4 sts plus 2)
Row 1 (RS) K2, *p2, k2; rep from * to end.
Row 2 P2, *k2, p2; rep from * to end.
Rep rows 1 and 2 for k2, p2 rib.

Seed stitch
(over an even number of sts)
Row 1 (RS) *K1, p1; rep from * to end.
Row 2 K the purl sts and p the knit sts.
Rep row 2 for seed st.

Back
With smaller needles, cast on 74 (86) sts. Work in k2, p2 rib for 1½"/4cm, inc 8 sts evenly spaced across last row and end with a WS row—82 (94) sts. Change to larger needles.

BEG CHART PATS
Row 1 (RS) Work in seed st over first 8 (14) sts, pm, work first 2 sts of chart I, then work 8-st rep twice, pm, work 30 sts of chart II, pm, work first 2 sts of chart III, then work 8-st rep twice, pm, work in seed st over last 8 (14) sts. Keeping 8 (14) sts each side in seed st, cont to foll charts I and III in this way to row 4, then rep rows 1–4 for cable pats, AT THE SAME TIME, work to row 8 of chart II, then rep

Gauges
20 sts and 32 rows to 4"/10cm over seed st using larger needles.
20 sts and 28 rows to 4"/10cm over St st using larger needles. *Take time to check gauges.*

Fisherman's Pullover

Chart I

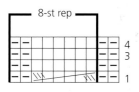

8-st rep

4
3
1

Chart II

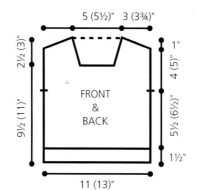

8
7
5
3
1

30 sts

Chart III

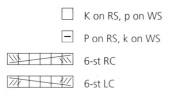

8-st rep

4
3
1

Stitch Key

☐ K on RS, p on WS

⊟ P on RS, k on WS

▨ 6-st RC

▨ 6-st LC

rows 1–8 for cable pat. Work even until piece measures 12 (14)"/30.5 (35.5)cm from beg, end with a WS row.

SHOULDER SHAPING
Bind off 18 (22) sts at beg of next 2 rows. Place rem 46 (50) sts on holder for back neck.

Front
Work same as back until piece measures 9½(11)"/24 (28)cm, end with a WS row.

NECK SHAPING
Next row (RS) Work across first 26 (30) sts, join another ball of yarn and bind off center 30 (34) stsfor front neck, work to end. Working both sides at once, work next row even.
Dec row (RS) With first ball of yarn, work to last 3 sts, k2tog, k1; with 2nd ball of yarn, k1, ssk, work to end. Work next row even. Rep last 2 rows 7 times more—18 (22) sts. Work until piece measures same length as back to shoulders, end with a WS row. Bind off each side. Sew shoulder seams. Place markers 4 (5)"/10 (12.5)cm

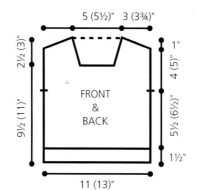

5 (5½)" 3 (3¾)"

2½ (3)"

9½ (11)"

FRONT & BACK

1"

4 (5)"

5½ (6½)"

1½"

11 (13)"

down from shoulders on back and fronts (measuring along seed st edges).

Sleeves
With RS facing and larger needles, pick up and k 62 (70) sts evenly spaced between armhole markers.
Set-up row (WS) Work in seed st over first 18 (22) sts, pm, k2, [p6, k2] 3 times, pm, work in seed st over last 18 (22) sts.

BEG CHART PAT
Row 1 (RS) Work in seed st over first 18 (22) sts, work first 2 sts of chart I, work 8-st rep 3 times, work in seed st over last 18 (22) sts.
Keeping 18 (22) sts each side in seed st, cont to foll chart in this way to row 4, then rep rows 1–4 for cable pat.

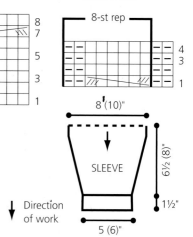

8'(10)"

SLEEVE

6½ (8)"

Direction of work

1½"

5 (6)"

Work even for 1"/2.5cm, end with a WS row. Dec 1 st each side on next row, then every 4th row 9(11)times more—42 (46) sts.
Work even until piece measures 6½ (8)"/16.5 (20.5)cm from beg, dec 8 sts evenly spaced across last row and end with a WS row—34 (38*) sts. Change to smaller needles. Work in k2, p2 rib for 1½"/4cm. Bind off loosely in rib.

Finishing
Block piece to measurements.

COLLAR
With RS facing and circular needle, pick up and k 28 (32) sts evenly spaced along right front neck edge, k 46 (50) sts from back neck holder, pick up and k 28 (32) sts evenly spaced along left front neck edge—102 (114) sts.
Beg with row 2, cont in k2, p2 rib for 3½ (4)"/9 (10)cm. Bind off loosely in rib. Lap right collar edge over left (for girls) or left collar edge over right (for boys). Sew side edges to bound-off edge of front neck. Sew side and sleeve seams. ■

Mosaic Blanket

Play up the colors of the nursery with this graphic warmer.

DESIGNED BY HEIDI KOZAR

EXPERIENCED

Knitted measurements
Approx 32" x 26½"/81cm x 67.5cm

Materials
■ 2 3½oz/100g balls (each approx 220yd/201m) of Cascade Yarns *220 Superwash* (superwash wool) each in #1911 turquoise heather (A), #1910 summer sky heather (B), #905 celery (C) and #1919 turtle (D)

■ Size 7 (4.5mm) circular needle, 36"/91cm length *or size to obtain gauge*

■ Bobbins

■ Stitch markers

Quick Tip
To help keep your place on the chart, use a ruler or large sticky note. Place the ruler above the row you are knitting, so you can see what you have already done.

Notes
1) Use a separate bobbin (or strand) of color for each color section.
2) When changing colors, pick up new color from under dropped color to prevent holes.

Blanket
With A, cast on 145 sts. Work in garter st (knit every row) for 16 rows, end with a WS row.

BEG CHART PAT
Row 1 (RS) K8 with A, pm, work sts 1–129 of chart, pm, k8 with A.
Row 2 K8 with A, sl marker, work sts 129–1 of chart, sl marker, k8 with A. Keeping 8 sts each side in garter st using A, cont to foll chart in this way to row 168, dropping markers on last row. With A, work in garter st for 16 rows. Bind off all sts loosely knitwise.

Finishing
Block piece lightly to measurements. ■

Gauge
18 sts and 30 rows to 4"/10cm over St st and chart pat using size 7 (4.5mm) circular needle. *Take time to check gauge.*

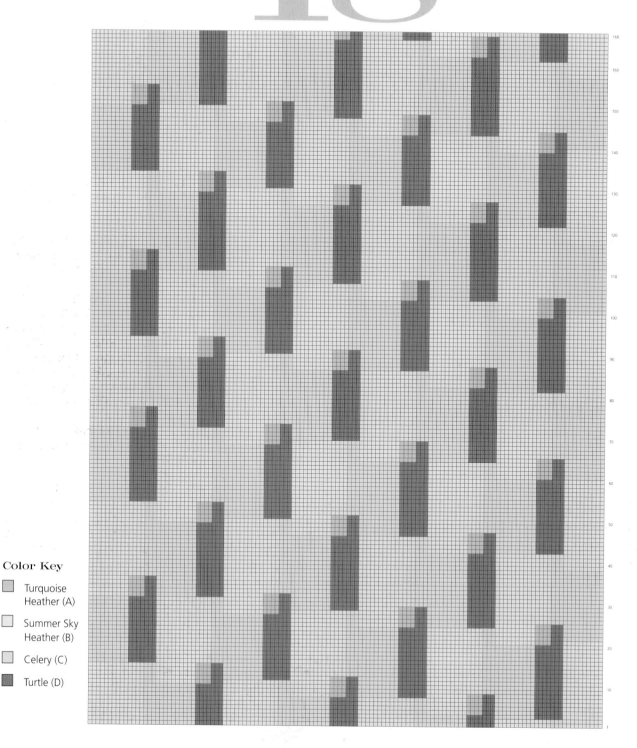

Color Key

- Turquoise Heather (A)
- Summer Sky Heather (B)
- Celery (C)
- Turtle (D)

Colorblock Cardigan

A graphic hue combination turns an otherwise basic sweater into a stylishly mod piece.

DESIGNED BY CHERYL MURRAY

INTERMEDIATE

Sizes

Instructions are written for size 6 months. Changes for 12 and 18 months are in parentheses.

Knitted measurements

Chest (closed) 22 (24, 26)"/56 (61, 66)cm
Length 12 (13, 14)"/30.5 (33, 35.5)cm
Upper arm 9 (10, 11)"/23 (25.5, 28)cm

Materials

- 1 (1, 2) 3½oz/100g balls (each approx 220yd/201m) of Cascade Yarns *220 Superwash* (superwash wool) each in #891 misty olive (A) and #910A winter white (B)
- 1 ball in #1940 peach (C)
- Size 7 (4.5mm) circular needle, 32"/81cm length *or size to obtain gauge*
- One pair size 7 (4.5mm) needles
- One set (5) size 7 (4.5mm) double-pointed needles (dpns)
- Stitch holders
- Stitch markers
- One 1⅛"/28mm button

Notes

1) Body and yoke are worked back and forth in one piece from the bottom up.
2) Sleeves are worked in the round.

K1, p1 rib

(over a multiple of 2 sts plus 1)
Row 1 (RS) K1, *p1, k1; rep from * to end.
Row 2 P1, *k1, p1; rep from * to end.
Rep rows 1 and 2 for k1, p1 rib.

Stripe pattern

Working in St st, *2 rnds C, 4 rnds B; rep from * (6 rnds) for stripe pat.

Body

With circular needle and A, cast on 119 (131, 139) sts. Work in k1, p1 rib for 4 rows, inc 1 (0, 1) st in center of last row—120 (131, 140) sts.

Next row (RS) K 30 (33, 35), pm, k 60 (65, 70), pm, k 30 (33, 35). Beg with a purl row, cont in St st until piece measures 3½"/9cm from beg, end with a WS row.

Dec row (RS) *Knit to 2 sts before marker, k2tog, sl marker, ssk; rep from * once more, knit to end. Rep dec row every 20th row once more—112 (123, 132) sts.

Work even until piece measures 7½ (8, 8½)"/19 (20.5, 21.5)cm from beg, end with a WS row.

DIVIDE FOR FRONTS AND BACK

Change to straight needles and B.
Next row (RS) K 28 (31, 33) sts, place sts on holder for right front, k 56 (61, 66) sts (back), leave rem 28 (31, 33) sts on needle for left front.

BACK

Beg with a purl row, cont in St st for

Gauge

20 sts and 28 rows to 4"/10cm over St st (k on RS, p on WS) using size 7 (4.5mm) circular needle. *Take time to check gauge.*

Colorblock Cardigan

5 rows, end with a WS row. Change to C. Work even until armhole measures 4½ (5, 5½)"/11.5 (12.5, 14)cm, end with a WS row. Bind off.

LEFT FRONT
Change to straight needles and B.
Next row (RS) K 28 (31, 33) sts. Cont in St st for 5 rows, end with a WS row. Change to C. Work even until armhole measures 2 (2½, 3)"/5 (6.5, 7.5)cm, end with a RS row.

NECK SHAPING
Bind off 6 (7, 7) sts from neck edge on next row once, then 2 sts from same edge once.
Dec row (RS) Knit to last 4 sts, k2tog, k2. Purl next row. Rep last 2 rows 4 times more. Work even on 15 (17, 19) sts until piece measures same length as back to shoulder, end with a WS row. Bind off.

RIGHT FRONT
Change to straight needles and B.
Next row (WS) P 28 (31, 33) sts on holder. Cont in St st for 4 rows, end with a WS row. Change to C. Work even until armhole measures 2 (2½, 3)"/5 (6.5, 7.5)cm, end with a WS row.

NECK SHAPING
Bind off 6 (7, 7) sts from neck edge on next row once, then 2 sts from same edge once.
Dec row (RS) K2, ssk, knit to end. Purl next row. Rep last 2 rows 4 times more. Work even on 15 (17, 19) sts until piece measures same length as back to shoulder, end with a WS row. Bind off. Sew shoulder seams.

SLEEVES
With RS facing, dpn and B, beg at underarm and pick up and k 46 (50, 56) sts evenly spaced around entire armhole edge. Divide sts evenly between 4 needles. Join and pm for beg of rnds. Work around in St st (knit every rnd) for 3 rnds. Cont in St st and stripe pat and work even for 0 (0, 2) rnds.
Dec rnd K2tog, knit to 2 sts before marker, ssk. Rep dec rnd every 5th (5th,

4th) rnd 7 (8, 10) times more. Work even on 30 (32, 34) sts until 15 (16, 17) stripes have been completed; piece should measures approx 6½ (7, 7½)"/16.5 (18, 19)cm from beg. Change to C (B, C).
Work around in k1, p1 rib for 4 rnds. Bind off in rib.

Finishing
Block piece to measurements.

I-CORD TRIM
With RS facing, circular needle and B, pick up and k 39 (41, 44) sts along right front edge to 2nd row of B stripe, fasten off yarn, skip next 3 rows of B stripe, cont to pick up and k 6 (9, 11) sts to neck edge, 20 (21, 21) sts along right neck edge to shoulder seam, 27 (29, 29) sts along back neck edge to left shoulder seam, 20 (21, 21) sts along left neck edge, then 47 (52, 57) sts along left front edge—159 (173, 183) sts. Fasten off yarn. Beg at bottom of right front, with dpn and B, cast on 3 sts. Attach I-cord as foll:
*Next row (RS) With 2nd dpn, k2, ssk with last st on dpn and next st on circular needle, do not turn. Slide sts back to beg of dpn to work next row from RS; rep from * to B stripe.
**Next row (RS) With 2nd dpn, k3, do not turn. Slide sts back to beg of dpn to work next row from RS; rep from ** for 1½"/4cm (button loop). Cont to attach I-cord, rep from * to * neck edge.
To turn corner, rep from ** to ** for 2 rows. Cont to attach I-cord, rep from * to * to opposite corner. To turn next corner, rep from ** to ** for 2 rows.
Cont to attach I-cord to end, rep from * to *. Bind off. Sew on button. ■

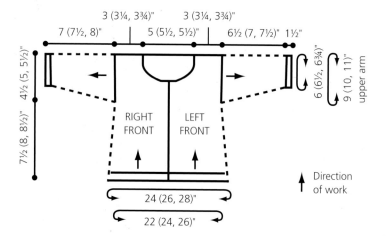

Leaf Lace Booties

With their pretty lace motif, these tiny shoes will look darling with a special-occasion dress.

DESIGNED BY JACQUELINE VAN DILLEN

■■■□
INTERMEDIATE

Size
Instructions are written for size 9 months.

Knitted measurements
Length of sole 5"/12.5cm
Width of foot 2½"/6.5cm

Materials
■ 1 3½oz/100g ball (approx 220yd /201m) of Cascade Yarns *220 Superwash* (superwash wool) in #831 rose
■ One pair size 4 (3.5mm) needles *or size to obtain gauge*
■ Two ½"/13mm buttons

Note
Booties are worked back and forth in one piece on two needles.

Left bootie
Beg at sole, cast on 36 sts.

HEEL AND TOE SHAPING
Row 1 (WS) Knit.
Row 2 K1, yo, k16, [yo, k1] twice, yo, k16, yo, k1—41 sts.
Row 3 Knit.
Row 4 K2, yo, k16, yo, k3, yo, k2, yo, k16, yo, k2—46 sts.
Row 5 Knit.
Row 6 K3, yo, k16, [yo, k4] twice, yo, k16, yo, k3—51sts.
Row 7 Knit.
Row 8 K4, yo, k16, yo, k6, yo, k5, yo, k16, yo, k4—56 sts.
Row 9 Knit.
Row 10 K5, yo, k16, [yo, k7] twice, yo, k16, yo, k5—61 sts.
Row 11 Knit.
Row 12 K22, yo, k9, yo, k8, yo, k22—64 sts.
Rows 13–23 Knit.

INSTEP
Note Sl sts at beg of rows wyib.
Row 1 (RS) K36, p2tog; turn.
Row 2 Sl 1 purlwise, k8, k2tog; turn.
Row 3 Sl 1 knitwise, p3, k1, yo, k1, p3, p2tog; turn.
Row 4 Sl 1 purlwise, k3, p3, k3, k2tog; turn.
Row 5 Sl 1 knitwise, p2, k2tog, yo, k1, yo, SKP, p2, p2tog; turn.
Row 6 Sl 1 purlwise, k2, p5, k2, k2tog; turn.
Row 7 Sl 1 knitwise, p1, k2tog, yo, k3, yo, SKP, p1, p2tog; turn.
Row 8 Sl 1 purlwise, k1, p7, k1, k2tog; turn.
Row 9 Sl 1 knitwise, k2tog, yo, k5, yo, SKP, p2tog; turn.
Row 10 Sl 1 purlwise, p9, k2tog; turn.
Row 11 Sl 1 knitwise, yo, k3, k3tog, k3, yo, p2tog; turn.
Row 12 Sl 1 purlwise, k1, p7, k1, k2tog; turn.
Row 13 Sl 1 knitwise, p1, yo, k2, k3tog, k2, yo, p1, p2tog; turn.
Row 14 Sl 1 purlwise, k2, p5, k2, k2tog; turn.

Gauge
22 sts and 44 rows to 4"/10cm over garter st using size 4 (3.5mm) needles.
Take time to check gauge.

Leaf Lace Booties

Yarn Smarts

Always buy all of the yarn you will need for a project at once and make sure all of the balls or skeins are from the same dye lot.

Row 15 Sl 1 knitwise, p2, yo, k1, k3tog, k1, yo, p2, p2tog; turn.
Row 16 Sl 1 purlwise, p9, k2tog; turn.
Row 17 Sl 1 knitwise, p3, yo, k3tog, yo, p3, p2tog; turn.
Row 18 Sl 1 purlwise, p9, k2tog; turn.
Row 19 Sl 1 knitwise, k2tog, k2, k2tog, k3, k2tog, knit to end—44 sts.

STRAP LOOP
Next row (WS) K 20, p4; turn. There will be 20 sts rem on RH needle.
Next row (RS) K4, turn.
Next row P4, turn. Rep last 2 rows until strap loop measures 2¼"/5.5cm from beg, end with a WS row.
Next row (RS) Bind off, leaving last st on needle. On left side edge of strap loop, pick up and k 10 sts evenly spaced, then knit 20 sts on LH needle—31 sts. Knit next row. Bind off knitwise. With RS facing, pick up and k 11 sts evenly spaced along right side edge of strap loop. Knit next row, including rem 20 sts—31 sts. Bind off knitwise. Sew sole and back heel seam. Fold strap loop in half to WS and sew top edge in place.

STRAP
Count 9 sts to the right of back seam and mark 9th st. Using cable cast-on method, cast on 22 sts, with RS facing and beg in marked st, pick up and k 9 sts to back seam, pick up and k next 9 sts, then cast on 4 sts—44 sts. Knit next 3 rows.
Next (buttonhole) row (RS) K2, yo, k2tog, knit to end. Knit next row. Bind off knitwise. Sew on button. Thread strap through loop.

Right bootie
Work same as left bootie to strap.

STRAP
Count 9 sts to the right of back seam and mark 9th st. Using cable cast-on method, cast on 4 sts, with RS facing and beg in marked st, pick up and k 9 sts to back seam, pick up and k next 9 sts, then cast on 22 sts—44 sts. Knit next 3 rows.
Next (buttonhole) row (RS) Knit to last 4 sts, k2tog, yo, k2. Knit next row. Bind off knitwise. Sew on button. Thread strap through loop. ■

Lace Motif Cardigan

This lively sweater features a pattern of eyelet diamonds. A seed stitch collar and borders complete the look.

DESIGNED BY DEBBIE O'NEILL

INTERMEDIATE

Sizes
Instructions are written for size 3 months. Changes for 6, 12 and 18 months are in parentheses.

Knitted measurements
Chest (closed) 19 (21, 23, 25)"/48 (53.5, 58.5, 63.5)cm
Length 10 (11, 12, 13)"/25.5 (28, 30.5, 33)cm
Upper arm 6 (7, 8, 9)"/15 (18, 20.5, 23)cm

Materials
- 2 (3, 3, 4) 3½oz/100g balls (each approx 220yd/201m) of Cascade Yarns *220 Superwash* (superwash wool) in #826 tangerine
- One pair size 7 (4.5mm) needles *or size to obtain gauge*
- Cable needle (cn)
- Stitch holder
- Stitch markers

Stitch glossary
3-st RC Sl next st to cn and hold to *back*, k2, k1 from cn.
3-st LC Sl next 2 sts to cn and hold to *front*, k1, k2 from cn.

Seed stitch
(over an odd number of sts)
Row 1 (RS) K1, *p1, k1; rep from * to end.
Row 2 K the purl sts and p the knit sts. Rep row 2 for seed st.

Back
Cast on 53 (57, 63, 69) sts. Work in seed st for 1"/2.5cm, end with a WS row. Cont in St st (knit on RS, purl on WS) and work even until piece measures 10 (11, 12, 13)"/25.5 (28, 30.5, 33)cm from beg, end with a WS row.

SHOULDER SHAPING
Bind off 16 (18, 21, 23) sts at beg of next 2 rows. Place rem 21 (21, 21, 23) sts on holder for back neck.

Right front
Cast on 27 (29, 33, 35) sts. Work in seed st for 1"/2.5cm, end with a WS row.

BEG CHART PAT
Row 1 (RS) Work in seed st over first 5 sts, pm, k2, pm, work chart over next 12 sts, k 8 (10, 14, 16).
Row 2 P 8 (10, 14, 16), sl marker, work chart over next 12 sts, sl marker, p2, sl marker, work in seed st over last 5 sts. Keeping sts at front edge in seed st, sts each side of chart in St st, cont to foll chart in this way to row 20, then rep rows 1–20 for lace pat.
Work even until piece measures 8 (9, 10, 11)"/20.5 (23, 25.5, 28)cm from beg, end with a WS row.

Gauge
22 sts and 30 rows to 4"/10cm over St st using size 7 (4.5mm) needles.
Take time to check gauge.

Lace Motif Cardigan

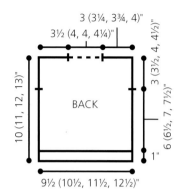

3 (3¼, 3¾, 4)"

3½ (4, 4, 4¼)"

3 (3½, 4, 4½)"

10 (11, 12, 13)"

BACK

6 (6½, 7, 7½)"

1"

9½ (10½, 11½, 12½)"

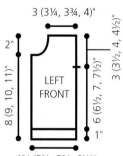

3 (3¼, 3¾, 4)"

2"

3 (3½, 4, 4½)"

8 (9, 10, 11)"

LEFT FRONT

6 (6½, 7, 7½)"

1"

4¾ (5¼, 5¾, 6¼)"

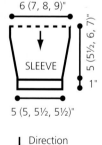

6 (7, 8, 9)"

5 (5½, 6, 7)"

SLEEVE

1"

5 (5, 5½, 5½)"

↓ Direction of work

NECK SHAPING
Bind off 5 (5, 6, 6) sts at beg of next row, then 3 sts at same (neck) edge once, 2 sts once, then 1 st once—16 (18, 21, 23) sts. Work even until piece measures same length as back to shoulder, end with a WS row. Bind off.

Left front
Cast on 27 (29, 33, 35) sts. Work in seed st for 1"/2.5cm, end with a WS row.

BEG CHART PAT
Note Chart pat begs on row 11 for left front.
Row 11 (RS) K 8 (10, 14, 16), pm, work chart over next 12 sts, pm, k2, pm, work in seed st over last 5 sts.
Row 12 Work in seed st over first 5 sts, sl marker, p2, sl marker, work chart over next 12 sts, sl marker, p 8 (10, 14, 16). Keeping sts at front edge in seed st, sts each side of chart in St st, cont to foll chart in this way to row 20, then rep rows 1–20 for lace pat.
Cont to work same as right front, reversing neck shaping. Sew shoulder seams. Place markers 3 (3½, 4, 4½)"/7.5 (9, 10, 11.5)cm down from shoulders on back and fronts.

Sleeves
With RS facing, pick up and k 35 (39, 45, 51) sts evenly spaced between markers. Purl next row. Cont to work even in St st for 1"/2.5cm, end with a WS row. Dec 1 st each side on next row, then every 10th (6th, 4th, 4th) row 2 (4, 6, 9) times more. Work even on 29 (29, 31, 31) sts until piece measures 5 (5½, 6, 7)"/12.5 (14, 15, 17.5)cm from beg, end with a WS row. Cont in seed st for 1"/2.5cm. Bind off in seed st.

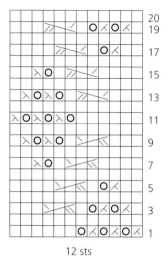

12 sts

Stitch Key

☐	K on RS, p on WS
O	Yo
⟋	K2tog
⟍	Ssk
3-st RC	3-st RC
3-st LC	3-st LC

Finishing
Block pieces to measurements.

NECKBAND
With RS facing, pick up and k 17 (17, 18, 18) sts evenly spaced along right front neck edge, k 21 (21, 21, 23) sts from back neck holder, pick up and k 17 (17, 18, 18) sts evenly spaced along left front neck edge—55 (55, 57, 59) sts. Work in seed st for 1"/2.5cm. Bind off in seed st. Sew side and sleeve seams. ■

52

Log Cabin Afghan

Individual knitted squares reminiscent of a treasured quilt motif
come together in a striking blanket.

DESIGNED BY DEBBIE O'NEILL

INTERMEDIATE

Knitted measurements
Approx 38" x 38"/96.5cm x 96.5cm

Materials
■ 3 3½oz/100g balls (each approx 220yd/201m) of Cascade Yarns *220 Superwash Quatro* (superwash wool) each in #1929 long beach (C) and #1935 lupin (E)

■ 2 balls each in #1931 summerdaze (B) and #1930 green tea (D)

■ 1 ball in #1933 chili pepper (A)

■ One pair size 7 (4.5mm) needles *or size to obtain gauge*

■ Size 7 (4.5mm) circular needle, 36"/91cm length

Squares (make 9)
COLOR A
With straight needles and A, cast on 17 sts. Work in garter st (knit every row) for 33 rows, end with a WS row. Cut A.

COLOR B
Change to color B and work in garter st for 22 rows. Bind off all sts knitwise, leaving last st on needle. Referring to diagram, turn to left side edge of strip, then pick up and k 27 sts along B and A sections—28 sts. Work in garter st for 21 rows. Bind off all sts knitwise, leaving last st on needle. Cut B.

COLOR C
Change to color C. Referring to diagram, turn to left, then pick up and k 27 sts along next edge—28 sts. Work in garter st for 21 rows. Bind off all sts knitwise, leaving last st on needle. Referring to diagram, turn to left, then pick up and k 38 sts along next edge—39 sts. Work in garter st for 21 rows. Bind off all sts knitwise, leaving last st on needle. Cut C.

COLOR D
Change to color D. Referring to diagram, turn to left, then pick up and k 38 sts along next edge—39 sts. Work in garter st 21 rows. Bind off all stitches knitwise, leaving last st on needle. Referring to diagram, turn to left, then pick up and k 49 sts along next edge—50 sts. Work in garter st for 21 rows. Bind off all sts knitwise, leaving last st on needle. Cut D.

COLOR E
Change to color E. Referring to diagram, turn to left, then pick up and k 49 sts along next edge—50 sts. Work in garter st 21 rows. Bind off all stitches knitwise, leaving last st on needle.

Gauge
20 sts and 40 rows to 4"/10cm over garter st using size 7 (4.5mm) needles.
Each square measures approx 12" x 12"/30.5cm x 30.5cm. *Take time to check gauge.*

Log Cabin Afghan

Referring to diagram, turn to left, then pick up and k 60 sts along last edge—61 sts. Work in garter st for 21 rows. Bind off all sts knitwise.

Finishing

Arrange 3 squares across by 3 squares high, making sure that top edges are at top. Sew squares tog. Block piece to 36" x 36"/91.5cm x 91.5cm.

Border

For first side, work as foll: with RS facing, circular needle and C, pick up and k 180 sts evenly spaced across right side edge. Work in garter st for 11 rows. Bind off all sts knitwise, leaving last st on needle. For second side, work as foll: turn to top edge and pick up and k 186 sts evenly spaced along top edge—187 sts. Work in garter st for 11 rows. Bind off all sts knitwise, leaving last st on needle. For third side, work as foll: turn to left side edge and pick up and k 192 sts evenly spaced across left side edge—193 sts. Work in garter st for 11 rows. Bind off all sts knitwise, leaving last st on needle. For fourth side, work as foll: turn to bottom edge and pick up and k 198 sts evenly spaced along bottom edge—199 sts. Work in garter st for 11 rows. Bind off all sts knitwise. ■

Square Diagram

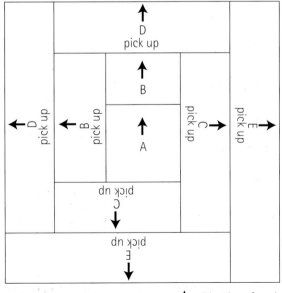

↑ = Direction of work

53

Tiny Tux

Dress your baby to the nines in this tuxedo vest sweater!
He'll fit right in at any holiday party.

DESIGNED BY LINDA MEDINA

INTERMEDIATE

Sizes

Instructions are written for size 6 months. Changes for 12 and 18 months are in parentheses.

Knitted measurements

Chest 23 (24½, 26)"/58.5 (62, 66)cm
Length 10½ (12¼, 13¾)"/26.5 (31, 35)cm
Upper arm 11"/28cm

Materials

■ 1 (2, 2) 3½oz/100g balls (each approx 220yd/200m) of Cascade Yarns *220 Superwash* (superwash wool) in #871 white (A)

■ 1 ball each in #1913 jet (B) and #893 ruby (C)

■ 1 skein 6-strand embroidery floss in dark burgundy

■ Size 5 (3.75mm) needles *or size to obtain gauge*

■ Size 5 (3.75mm) circular needle, 16"/40cm long

■ Four ⅜"/10mm flat white buttons for "shirt"

■ Three ⅜"/10mm black shank-type buttons for "vest"

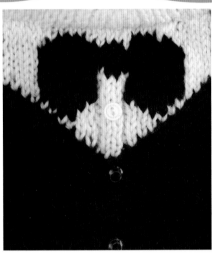

■ Two ½"/13mm flat black buttons for placket

■ One ½"/13mm flat white button for placket

■ 2 small stitch holders

■ Tapestry needle

■ Sewing needle and matching thread

Note

"Bow tie" may be worked in intarsia or duplicate stitch. "Shadow" on tie is worked with embroidery floss in duplicate stitch.

Stitch glossary

2-st one-row buttonhole Bring yarn to front and slip the next st, bring yarn to back, *sl 1, pass previously slipped st over it; rep from * once, slip last st back to left-hand needle and turn. Using cable cast-on wyib, cast on 3 sts and turn. Slip first st from left-hand needle and pass last cast-on st over it.

M1 Insert LH needle from back to front under the strand between last st worked and the next st on the LH needle. Knit into the front loop to twist the st.

Front

With straight needles and A, cast on 63 (67, 71) sts.
Row 1 (RS) *K1, p1; rep from * to last st, k1.
Row 2 P1, *k1, p1; rep from * to end.
Rep rows 1 and 2 once more, inc 1 st in center of last row—64 (68, 72) sts.

BEG CHART PAT
Note Attach a second ball of B when beg the lower points of vest, working with both balls through row 22.
Work in St st (knit on RS, purl on WS) in chart as foll:
For size 6 mos only, beg with row 13 and work through row 44.

Gauge

22 sts and 28 rows to 4"/10cm over St st. *Take time to check gauge.*

Tiny Tux

For size 12 mos only, work rows 1–44 once.

For size 18 mos only, work rows 1–40 once, then rows 31–44 once.
Piece measures approx 5 (6¾, 8¼)"/12.5 (17, 21)cm from beg.

ARMHOLE SHAPING
Cont working chart, bind off 3 (4, 5) sts at beg of rows 45 and 46, then bind off 2 sts at beg of rows 47 and 48.
Rows 49 and 51 Dec 1 st at each side of row—50 (52, 54) sts.
Rows 50 and 52 Purl.

NECK SHAPING
Cont working chart through row 74.
Row 75 K13 (14, 15) B, k5 A, attach a second ball of A and bind off 14 sts, k5 A, k13 (14, 15) B.

RIGHT SHOULDER
Row 76 (WS) P13 (14, 15) B, p5 A.
Row 77 With A, bind off 3, k2, k to end with B.
Row 78 P13 (14, 15) B, p2 A.
Row 79 With A, bind off 1, k to end with B.
Row 80 P13 (14, 15), p1 A.
Row 81 Bind off 1, k to end with B.
Row 82 P13 (14, 15) B.
Place sts on holder.

LEFT SHOULDER
Row 76 (WS) With A, bind off 3 sts, p1, p to end with B.
Row 77 K13 (14, 15) B, k2 A.
Row 78 With A, bind off 1, p to end with B.
Row 79 K13 (14, 15) B, k1 A.
Row 80 Bind off 1, p to end with B.
Row 81 K13 (14, 15) B.

Row 82 P13 (14, 15) B.
Place sts on holder.

Back
With straight needles and A, cast on 63 (67, 71) sts.
Work 4 rows rib same as front—64 (68, 72) sts.
Work in St st for 12 (24, 24) rows.
Change to B.
Work in St st for 20 (20, 30) rows.
Note Cont with B to end of piece.

ARMHOLE SHAPING
Bind off 3 (4, 5) sts at beg of next 2 rows, 2 sts at beg of next 2 rows.
Dec 1 st each side of every other row twice—50 (52, 54) sts.
Work 8 rows in St st.

PLACKET SHAPING
Next row (RS) K23 (24, 25), attach a second ball of B and bind off 4 sts, k to end.
Working both sides at the same time, work 17 rows in St st.

NECK SHAPING
RIGHT SIDE
Row 1 (RS) Knit.
Row 2 Bind off 7 sts, p to end.
Row 3 Knit.
Row 4 Bind off 3 sts, p to end.
Do not cut yarn.

LEFT SIDE
Row 1 (RS) Bind off 7 sts, k to end.
Row 2 Purl.
Row 3 Bind off 3 sts, k to end.
Row 4 Purl.

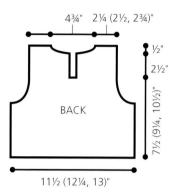

BACK

4¾" 2¼ (2½, 2¾)"
½"
2½"
7½ (9¼, 10½)"
11½ (12¼, 13)"

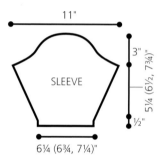

SLEEVE

11"
3"
5¼ (6½, 7¾)"
½"
6¼ (6¾, 7¼)"

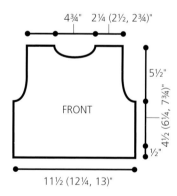

FRONT

4¾" 2¼ (2½, 2¾)"
5½"
4½ (6¼, 7¾)"
½"
11½ (12¼, 13)"

Do not cut yarn.
Using 3-needle bind-off, join front and back shoulders.

BACK PLACKET
BUTTON BAND
With RS facing and B, pick up and k 15 sts along left placket edge.
Row 1 (WS) P1, *k1, p1; rep from * to end.
Row 2 K1, *p1, k1; rep from * to end.
Rep rows 1 and 2 twice more. Bind off in rib, leaving about an 8"/20.5cm tail.

BUTTONHOLE BAND
With RS facing and B, pick up and k 15 sts along right placket edge.
Rows 1 and 3 (WS) P1, *k1, p1; rep from * to end.
Row 2 K1, *p1, k1; rep from * to end.
Row 4 [K1, p1] twice, make 2-st one-row buttonhole, p1, k1, p1, make 2-st one-row buttonhole, p1, k1.
Rows 5 and 6 Rep rows 1 and 2.
Bind off in rib.

Overlap with buttonhole band on top. Using tail from button band, sew lower edges of bands and placket opening together.

NECKBAND
With RS facing, circular needle and A, starting at edge of button band, pick up and k 71 sts evenly around neck opening.
Row 1 (WS) P1, *k1, p1; rep from * to end.

Row 2 K1, *p1, k1; rep from * to last 5 sts, make 2-st one-row buttonhole, p1, k1.
Row 3 Rep row 1.
Bind off in rib.
Sew white ½"/13mm button to neckband, and 2 black ½"/13mm buttons to button band.

Sleeves
With A, cast on 35 (37, 39) sts.
Row 1 (RS) K1, *p1, k1; rep from * to end.
Row 2 P1, *k1, p1; rep from * to end.
Rep rows 1 and 2 once more.
Row 5 Knit.
Row 6 Purl.
Inc row (RS) K1, M1, k to last 2 sts, M1, k1.
Rep inc row every 2nd (2nd, 4th) row 12 (11, 10) times more—61 sts.
Work even in St st until sleeve measures 5¾ (7, 8¼)"/14.5 (17.5, 21)cm from beg, end with a WS row.

CAP SHAPING
Bind off 3 (4, 5) sts at beg of next 2 rows, 2 sts at beg of next 2 rows.
Dec 1 st each side every other row 7 times.
Bind off 3 sts at beg of next 2 rows, 4 (3, 2) sts at beg of next 2 rows.
Bind off rem 23 sts.

Finishing
Block pieces lightly to measurements.
Set in sleeves. Sew side and sleeve seams.
Work "bow tie" in duplicate stitch if needed. With embroidery floss, work bow tie shadow in duplicate st and steam lightly.
Sew shirt and vest buttons in place with matching sewing thread. ■

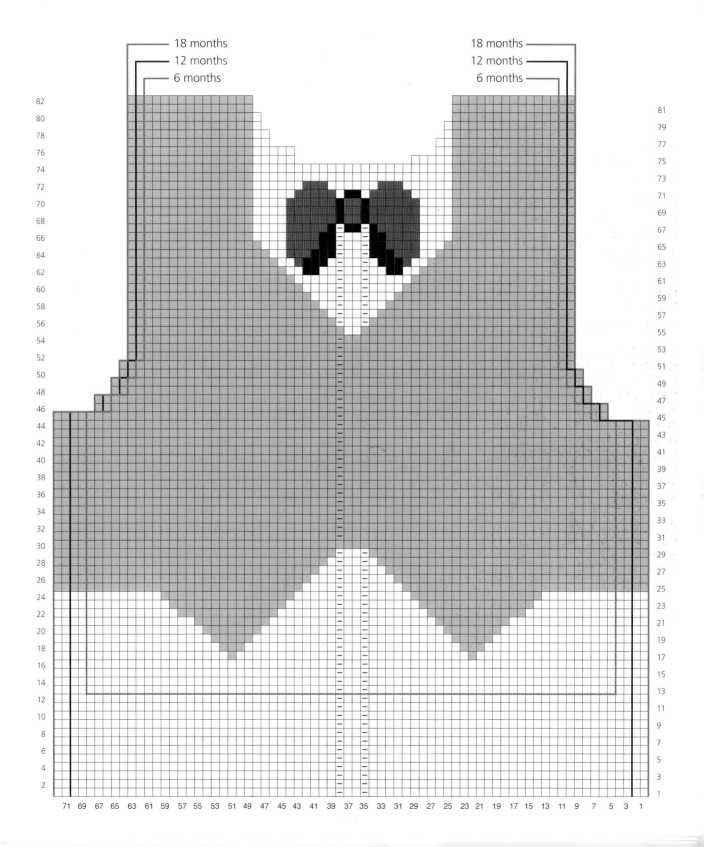

Twisted Rib Cardigan

Add a touch of sophistication to baby's wardrobe with this classic sweater.
The ribbing in the bodice gives it flair.

DESIGNED BY JEANNIE CHIN

■■■■
EXPERIENCED

Sizes
Instructions are written for size 3 months. Changes for 6, 12 and 18 months are in parentheses.

Knitted measurements
Chest (closed) 21 (22, 23, 23½)"/53.5 (56, 58.5, 59.5)cm
Length 10¼ (11, 11¾, 12¼)"/26 (28, 30, 31)cm
Upper arm 9½ (10, 10½, 11¾)"/24 (25.5, 26.5, 30)cm

Materials
■ 3 (3, 4, 5) 3½ oz/100g balls (each approx 220yd/201m) of Cascade Yarns *220 Superwash* (superwash wool) in #837 berry pink
■ One pair size 6 (4mm) needles *or size to obtain gauge*
■ Size E-4 (3.5mm) crochet hook
■ Three ⅝"/16mm buttons
■ Stitch markers

Twisted rib (multiple of 2 sts plus 1)
Row 1 (RS) K1, *p1 tbl, k1 tbl; rep from *, end p1 tbl, k1.
Row 2 P1, *k1 tbl, p1 tbl; rep from * end k1 tbl, p1.
Rep rows 1 and 2 for twisted rib.

Back
Cast on 69 (71, 73, 75) sts. Purl next 2 rows. Beg with a knit row, cont in St st (knit on RS, purl on WS) until piece measures 5¾ (6¼, 6¾, 6¾)"/14.5 (16, 17, 17)cm from beg, end with a RS row.
Next (inc) row (WS) Purl across, inc 18 sts evenly spaced—87 (89, 91, 93) sts.

BODICE
Cont in twisted rib and work even for 2 rows. Piece should measure approx 6 (6¼, 7, 7)"/15 (16.5, 18, 18)cm from beg.

ARMHOLE AND NECK SHAPING
Bind off 2 sts beg next 2 rows—83 (85, 87, 89) sts.
Note Work dec rows for RS and WS as foll:
Dec row 1 (RS) K1, k2tog tbl, work in twisted rib to last 3 sts, k2tog, k1.
Dec row 2 (WS) P1, p2tog, work in twisted rib to last 3 sts, p2tog tbl, p1.

FOR SIZE 3 MONTHS ONLY: [Work 26 dec rows. AT THE SAME TIME, when armhole measures 3½"/9cm, shape back neck as foll: bind off center 17 sts, then bind off from each neck edge 4 sts once, then 2 sts once. Fasten off last st each side.

FOR SIZES 6 AND 12 MONTHS ONLY
[Work 6 dec rows, work next row even] 2 (4) times, then work 14 (2) dec rows

more. AT THE SAME TIME, when armhole measures approx 3¾ (4¼)"/9.5 (11)cm, shape back neck as foll: bind off center 17 sts, then bind off from each neck edge 5 (6) sts once, then 2 sts once. Fasten off last st each side.

FOR SIZE 18 MONTHS ONLY
[Work 6 dec rows, work next row even] 3 times, [work 4 dec rows, then work next row even] twice, work 1 dec row more, then work next row even. AT THE SAME TIME, when armhole measures approx 4¾"/12cm, shape back neck as foll: bind off center 17 sts, then bind off from each neck edge 6 sts once, then 2 sts once. Fasten off last st each side.

Left front
Cast on 41 (41, 43, 43) sts. Purl next 2 rows.
Row 1 (RS) K 31 (31, 33, 33), pm, k4, sl 1, k5 (button band).
Row 2 Purl. Rep rows 1 and 2 until piece measures 5¾ (6¼, 6¾, 6¾)"/14.5 (16, 17, 17)cm from beg, end with a RS row.
Next (inc) row (WS) P10, sl marker, purl to end, inc 8 (10, 10, 10) sts evenly spaced across—49 (51, 53, 53) sts.

BODICE
Cont in twisted rib and button band as foll:
Row 1 (RS) K1, *p1 tbl, k1 tbl; rep from * to marker, sl marker, k4, sl 1, k5.

Gauges
22 sts and 30 rows to 4"/10cm over St st using size 6(4mm) needles. 32 sts and 28 rows to 4"/10cm over twisted rib using size 6(4mm) needles.

Twisted Rib Cardigan

Row 2 P10, sl marker, *p1 tbl, k1 tbl; rep from *, end p1. Piece should measure same length as back to underarm.

ARMHOLE AND NECK SHAPING
Bind off 2 sts at beg of next row—47 (49, 51, 51) sts.
Note Work dec rows for RS and WS as foll:
Dec row 1 (RS) K1, k2tog tbl, work in twisted rib to last 10 sts, sl marker, k4, sl 1, k5.
Dec row 2 (WS) P10, sl marker, work in twisted rib to last 3 sts, p2tog tbl, p1.
FOR 3 AND 6 MONTHS SIZES ONLY
Work 27 (29) dec rows. AT THE SAME TIME, when armhole measures approx 2½ (2¾)"/6.5 (7)cm, shape front neck as foll: at neck edge, bind off 13 sts once, 3 sts once, 2 sts once, then dec 1 st from neck edge once. Fasten off last st.

FOR 12 AND 18 MONTHS SIZE ONLY
[Work 6 dec rows, work next row even] 2 (4) times, then 14 (2) dec rows. AT THE SAME TIME, when armhole measures approx 2¾ (3)"/7 (7.5)cm, shape front neck as foll: at neck edge, bind off 14 sts once, 3 sts once, 2 sts twice, then dec 1 st from neck edge every row 3 times. Fasten off last st. Place markers for 3 buttons on button band, with the first ¼"/.5cm from beg of bodice, the last ¼"/.5cm from neck edge and the other evenly spaced between.

Right front
Cast on 41(41,43,43) sts. Purl next 2 rows.
Row 1 (RS) K5, sl 1, k4 (buttonhole band), pm, k 31 (31, 33, 33).
Row 2 Purl. Rep rows 1 and 2 until piece measures 5¾ (6¼, 6¾, 6¾)"/14.5 (16, 17, 17)cm from beg, end with a RS row.
Next (inc) row (WS) Purl to marker, inc 8 (10, 10, 10) sts evenly spaced, sl marker, p10—49 (51, 53, 53) sts. Cont to work same as left front, reversing all shaping and working buttonholes opposite

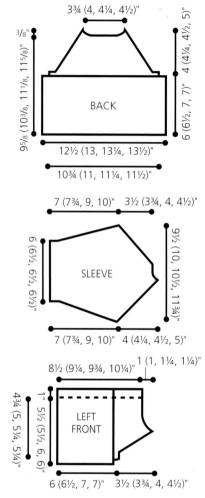

BACK

3¾ (4, 4¼, 4½)"

3/8"

9⅝ (10⅜, 11⅛, 11⅝)"

4 (4¼, 4½, 5)"

6 (6½, 7, 7)"

12½ (13, 13¼, 13½)"

10¾ (11, 11¼, 11½)"

SLEEVE

7 (7¾, 9, 10)" 3½ (3¾, 4, 4½)"

6 (6½, 6½, 6½)"

9½ (10, 10½, 11¾)"

7 (7¾, 9, 10)" 4 (4¼, 4½, 5)"

LEFT FRONT

8½ (9¼, 9¾, 10¼)" 1 (1, 1¼, 1¼)"

4¾ (5, 5¼, 5¼)"

1" 5½ (5½, 6, 6)"

6 (6½, 7, 7)" 3½ (3¾, 4, 4½)"

markers as foll:
Next (buttonhole) row (RS) K1, k2tog, yo, k2, sl 1, k2, yo, k2tog, work in twisted rib to end.

Left sleeve
Cast on 34 (36, 36, 36) sts. Purl next 2 rows. Beg with a knit row, cont in St st for 4 rows, end with a WS row.
Inc row (RS) K1, M1 (see page 4), knit to last st, M1, k1. Rep inc row every 4th row

8 (9, 10, 13) times more—52 (56, 58, 64) sts. Work even until piece measures 7 (7¾, 9, 10)"/18 (19.5, 23, 25.5)cm from beg, end with a WS row.

CAP SHAPING
Note Work dec rows on RS and WS same as back.

FOR ALL SIZES: [Work 3 dec rows, then work next row even] 6 (6, 5, 7) times, work 3 (5, 9, 6) dec rows more—10 sts.

FOR SIZE 3 MONTHS ONLY
Row 1 (WS) Bind off 4 sts, work to last 3 sts, p2tog tbl, p1—5 sts.
Row 2 K1, k2tog tbl, k2tog—3 sts.
Row 3 P2tog tbl, p1. Bind off rem 2 sts.

FOR SIZE18 MONTHS ONLY
Work 1 row even.
FOR SIZES 6, 12 AND 18 MONTHS ONLY
Row 1 (WS) Bind off 5 sts, work to last 3 sts, p2tog tbl, p1—4 sts.
Row 2 K1, k2tog tbl, k1. Bind off rem 3 sts.

Right sleeve
Work as for left sleeve, reversing cap shaping.

Finishing
Block pieces to measurements; do not block ribbing. Split yarn into 2-ply strands for sewing. Sew raglan armhole seams, side and sleeve seams. Fold buttonhole band and button band in half to WS along sl st ridge. Sew side and bottom edges in place. Whipstitch edges of buttonholes tog.

NECK EDGING
With RS facing and crochet hook, join yarn with a sl st left neck edge.
Row 1 (RS) Working from left to right, sc evenly along entire neck edge, working through both layers of front bands. Fasten off. Sew on buttons. ■

55

Preppy Cardigan

Your little scholar will be ready to hit the books (or the playground) in this spiffy sweater.

DESIGNED BY LEE GANT

INTERMEDIATE

Sizes

Instructions are written for size 6 months. Changes for 12 and 18 months are in parentheses.

Knitted measurements

Chest (buttoned) 20 (22, 24)"/51 (56, 61)cm
Length 12¼ (13¼, 14½)"/31 (33.5, 37)cm
Upper arm 7¼ (8½, 9)"/18.5 (21, 23)cm

Materials

- 2 (3, 3) 3½oz/100g balls (each approx 220 yd/201m) of Cascade Yarns *220 Superwash* in #891 misty olive (MC)
- 1 ball in #871 white (CC)
- Size 4 (3.5mm) circular needle, 24"/60cm long
- Size 6 (4mm) circular needle, 24"/60cm long, *or size to obtain gauge*
- Cable needle
- Tapestry needle
- Stitch markers
- Stitch holders or waste yarn
- 5 (5, 6) ⅝"/16mm buttons

Stitch glossary

C4B Slip 2 sts to cn and hold to *back*, k2, k2 from cn.
C4F Slip 2 sts to cn and hold to *front*, k2, k2 from cn.
Kfb Knit into the front and the back of st.
M1 Insert LH needle from back to front under the strand between last st worked and the next st on the LH needle. Knit into the front loop to twist the st.

Yoke

With MC and larger needle, cast on 42 (46, 54) sts for neck edge.
Set-up row (WS) P1 for right front, pm, p8 (10, 12) for right sleeve, pm, p24 (24, 28) for back, pm, p8 (10, 12) for left sleeve, pm, p1 for left front.
Row 1 (RS) [Kfb, slip marker (sm), kfb, k to 1 st before next marker] 3 times, kfb, sm, kfb—50 (54, 62) sts.
Row 2 and all WS rows Purl.
Row 3 K1, M1, [kfb, sm, kfb, k to 1 st before next marker] 3 times, kfb, sm, kfb, k to last st, M1, k1—60 (64, 72) sts.
Row 5 K1, M1, [k to 1 st before next marker, kfb, sm, kfb] 4 times, k to last st, M1, k1—70 (74, 82) sts.
Row 6 Purl.

SET UP CABLED RAGLAN SHAPING
Row 1 (RS) K1, M1, [C4B, kfb, sm, kfb, C4F, k to 5 sts before next marker] 3 times, C4B, kfb, sm, kfb, C4F, M1, k1—80 (84, 92) sts.
Row 2 and all WS rows Purl.
Row 3 [Work to 1 st before next marker, kfb, sm, kfb] 4 times, work to end—88 (92, 100) sts.
Row 5 (RS) K1, M1, [k to 5 sts before next marker, C4B, kfb, sm, kfb, C4F] 4 times, k to last st, M1, k1—11 sts each front, 20 (22, 24) sts each sleeve, 36 (36,

Gauge

22 sts and 28 rows = 4"/10cm over St st (k on RS, p on WS) using larger needle. *Take time to check gauge.*

Preppy Cardigan

40) sts back—98 (102, 110) sts. Cont as established, working M1 incs at beg and end of every 4th row 2 (3, 5) times more then every 6th row 2 (2, 1) times more, twist cables every 4th row 4 (5, 6) times more, and kfb incs every RS row 10 (12, 13) times more, and AT SAME TIME when back measures 3 (3½, 4)"/ 7.5 (9, 10)cm from beg, end with RS row and work 1-row stripe as foll:
Next row (WS) With CC, purl 1 row. Sl sts back to other end of needle and purl next row on WS with MC. Cont as established until all incs are done—25 (28, 30) sts each front, 40 (46, 50) sts each sleeve, 56 (60, 66) sts for back, end with a WS row—186 (208, 226) sts.

DIVIDE FOR SLEEVES
Next row (RS) K 25 (28, 30) left front sts, and place on holder, k 40 (46, 50) left sleeve sts, place rem sts on second holder.

SLEEVES
Work left sleeve only as foll: **Next row (WS)** Purl. Work 2 more rows in St st.
Next (dec) row (RS) K1, ssk, k to last 3 sts, k2tog, k1—38 (44, 48) sts. Cont in St st and rep dec row every 8th (8th, 6th) row 4 (5, 7) times more—30 (34, 34) sts. Work even until sleeve measures 5½ (6, 7)"/12.5 (14, 18)cm from underarm, end with a WS row.

CUFF
Change to smaller needles and CC. Beg and end with k2 and work in k2, p2 rib until cuff measures 1¼"/3cm, end with a WS row.
Next row (RS) With MC, k 1 row. Sl sts back to other end of needle and k next

row on RS with CC. Cont in rib until cuff measures 2"/5cm. Bind off loosely in rib.

RIGHT SLEEVE
Place 40 (46, 50) right sleeve sts back on needle, ready for RS row. Rejoin yarn, k 1 row. Complete same as left sleeve.

BODY
Place right front, back and left front sts on needle, ready for RS row—106 (116, 126) sts. Rejoin MC and work in St st until body measures 5 (5½, 6)"/12.5 (14, 15)cm from underarm, and inc 0 (2, 0) sts evenly across last WS row—106 (118, 126) sts.

WAISTBAND RIBBING
With smaller needles and CC, beg and end with k2, and work in k2, p2 rib with 1-row MC stripe same as sleeve cuff.

FRONT AND NECK BANDS
With RS facing, CC and smaller needle, pick up and knit 41 (44, 50) sts along right front edge to neck shaping, 20 (23,

25) sts along right neck edge, 8 (10, 12) sts along shoulder, 24 (24, 28) sts along back neck, 8 (10, 12) sts along shoulder, 20 (23, 25) sts along left neck edge and shoulder, 41 (44, 50) sts along left front edge—162 (178, 202) sts.
Next row (WS) P2, *k2, p2; rep from * to end. Work in k2, p2 rib for 2 more rows.

BUTTONHOLES
Place markers on right front band for 5 (5, 6) buttonholes (mark 2 sts), the first one after 4 sts from lower edge, the last one at beg of neck shaping, and the others spaced evenly between.
Buttonhole row (RS) *Work in rib to next buttonhole marker, yo, k2tog; rep from * for each marker, work in rib to end. Work 3 more rows in rib as established. With MC, bind off loosely knitwise.

Finishing
Sew sleeve seams. Sew buttons to correspond with buttonholes. Block lightly to measurements. ■

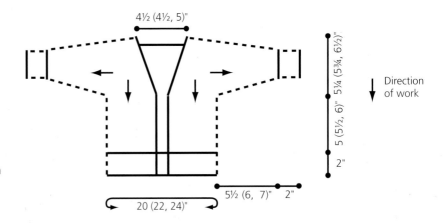

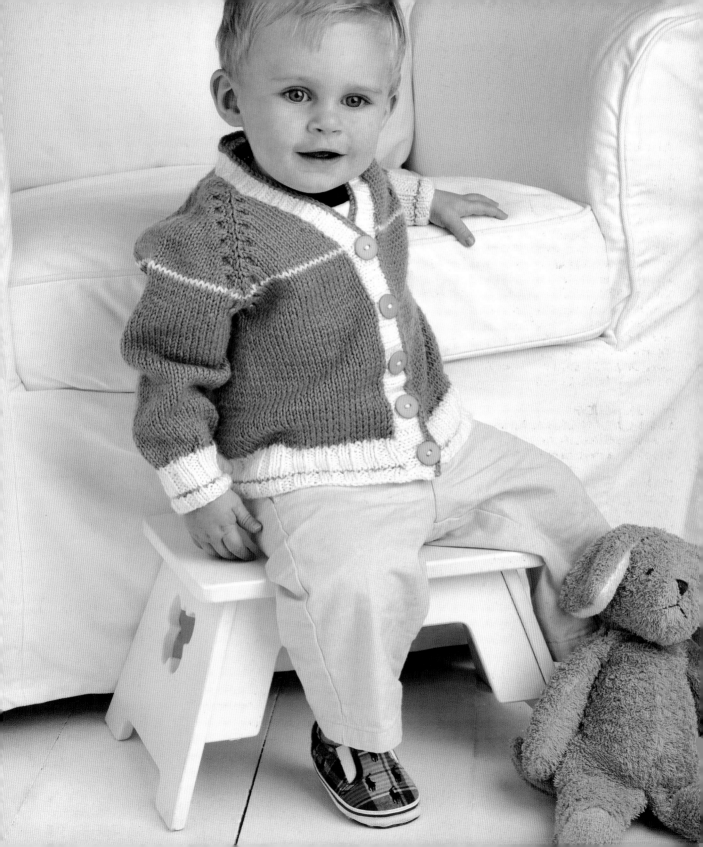

56

Garter Ridge Earflap Hat

Braided trimmings and a crocheted edging put an extra-special spin on a traditional head-hugger.

DESIGNED BY ERSSIE MAJOR

INTERMEDIATE

Size

Instructions are written for size 6–12 months.

Knitted measurements

Head circumference 16"/40.5cm
Depth 6"/15cm (excluding earflaps)

Materials

- 1 3½oz/100g ball (approx 220yd/201m) of Cascade Yarns *220 Superwash* (superwash wool) each in #1946 silver grey (MC) and #816 grey (CC)
- Size 7 (4.5mm) circular needle, 16"/40cm length *or size to obtain gauge*
- One set (5) size 7 (4.5mm) double-pointed needles (dpns)
- Size F-5 (3.75mm) crochet hook
- Stitch holders
- Stitch markers

Earflaps (make 2)

With dpn and MC, cast on 4 sts. Work back and forth on two needles as foll:
Row 1 (RS) Sl 1 purlwise, k1, yo (eyelet for braid), k2—5 sts. **Row 2** Sl 1 purlwise, k1, k2tog, k1—4 sts. **Row 3** Sl 1 purlwise, M1 (see p. 4), knit to last st, M1, k1—6 sts.
Row 4 Sl 1 purlwise, knit to end.

Rep rows 3 and 4 seven times more—20 sts. Place sts on holder.

Hat

With circular needle and MC, and beg at center back of hat, cast on 6 sts using knitted or cable cast-on method; with RS facing, knit 20 sts from first earflap holder, cast on 20 sts, knit 20 sts from 2nd earflap holder, then cast on 6 sts—72 sts. Join and pm for beg of rnds. Purl next rnd. Cont in garter st (knit 1 rnd, purl 1 rnd) for 8 rnds. Cont in St st (knit every rnd) until piece measures 5"/12.5cm from cast-on edge of hat.

CROWN SHAPING

Note Change to dpns (dividing sts evenly between 4 needles) when there are too few sts to work with circular needle.
Dec rnd 1 *K7, k2tog; rep from * around—64 sts. **Dec rnd 2** *K6, k2tog; rep from * around—56 sts. **Dec rnd 3** *K5, k2tog; rep from * around—48 sts. **Dec rnd 4** *K4, k2tog; rep from * around—40 sts. **Dec rnd 5** *K3, k2tog; rep from * around—32 sts. **Dec rnd 6** *K2, k2tog; rep from * around—24 sts. **Dec rnd 7** *K1, k2tog; rep from * around—16 sts. **Dec rnd 8** [K2tog] 8 times—8 sts. Cut yarn, leaving an 8"/20.5cm tail, and thread through rem sts. Pull tog tightly and secure end.

Finishing

EDGING

With RS facing and crochet hook, join CC with a sl st in center back bottom edge of hat. **Rnd 1 (RS)** Ch 1, making sure that work lies flat, sc evenly around entire bottom edge of hat including earflaps, join with a sl st in first sc. Fasten off.

TOP BRAID

Cut twenty-four 10"/25.5cm lengths of CC. Wrap a 12"/30.5cm strand of CC several times around center of strands, then knot to secure this strand. Do *not* trim off strand; it will be used to sew braid to hat. Fold strands in half and even up ends—48 strands. Divide strands into three 16-strand bundles. Braid to within 1¼"/3cm of ends, then wrap a 12"/30.5cm strand of CC several times around braid to secure. Trim ends evenly. Sew braid to center top of hat.

EARFLAP BRAID (make 2)

Cut twenty-four 10"/25.5cm lengths of CC. Use crochet hook to draw strands through eyelet at bottom of earflap. Fold strands in half and even up ends—48 strands. With RS of earflap facing, divide strands into three 16-strand bundles. Braid to within 1¼"/3cm of ends, then wrap a 12"/30.5cm strand of CC several times around braid to secure. Trim ends. ■

Gauge

18 sts and 26 rnds to 4"/10cm over St st using size 7 (4.5mm) circular needle. *Take time to check gauge.*

57

Criss-Cross Booties

The cross-over straps on these colorful slippers help them stay on the little one's active feet.

DESIGNED BY ANGELA JUERGENS

Size
Instructions are written for size 6 months.

Knitted measurements
Length of sole 4½"/11.5cm
Width of foot 2¼"/6cm

Materials
■ 1 3½oz/100g ball (approx 220yd/201m) of Cascade Yarns *220 Superwash* (superwash wool) each in #811 como blue (MC), #822 pumpkin (A), #812 turquoise (B) and #877 tangerine (C)

■ Size 4 (3.5mm) circular needle, 24"/61cm length *or size to obtain gauge*

■ Crochet hook size B-1 (2.25mm)

■ Four ⅝"/16mm buttons

Note Booties are made in one piece, including straps.

Stitch glossary
kf&b Inc 1 by knitting into the front and back of the next st.

Booties (make 2)
Beg at sole, with MC, cast on 40 sts using long-tail cast-on method. Do not join. Work back and forth as foll:
Row 1 (WS) With MC , knit.

BOTTOM OF HEEL AND TOE SHAPING
Row 2 (RS) With MC, kf&b, k18, M1, k2, M1 (see p. 4), k18, kf&b—44 sts. **Row 3** With MC, knit. **Row 4** With MC, kf&b, k19, M1, k4, M1, k19, kf&b—48 sts. **Row 5** With MC, knit. **Row 6** With MC, kf&b, k20, M1, k1, M1, k4, M1, k1, M1, k20, kf&b—54 sts. **Row 7** With MC, knit. **Row 8** With MC, kf&b, k21, M1, k1, M1, k8, M1, k1, M1, k21, kf&b—60 sts. **Row 9** With MC, knit. **Row 10 (RS)** With MC, k3, *with A, k2, with MC, k2; rep from *, end, with MC, k1. **Row 11** Rep row 10, making sure to carry color not in use on WS. **Rows 12–15** With A, knit. **Row 16** With B, k2, *sl 1 purlwise wyib, with B, k1; rep from * to end. **Rows 17–19** With B, knit. **Row 20** With C, k2, *sl 1 purlwise wyib, with C, k1; rep from * to end. **Row 21** With C, knit.

TOP OF TOE SHAPING
Row 22 With C, k18, [ssk] 6 times, [k2tog] 6 times, k18—48 sts. **Row 23** With C, knit. **Row 24 (RS)** With MC, k3, *with C, k2, with MC, k2; rep from *, end with MC, k1. **Row 25** Rep row 24, making sure to carry color not in use on WS. **Row 26** With MC, knit.

TOP OF TOE OPENING
Row 27 (WS) With MC, k11, bind off next 26 sts very tightly to gather edge, knit to end—11 sts each side of bound-off sts. Turn piece to RS. Slide 11 sts from left half of bootie to tip of RH needle, then transfer these sts to LH needle. Side edges of bootie that form the center back seam now meet. Cut yarn, leaving a long tail for sewing.

STRAPS
Row 1 With MC, cast on 11 sts to RH needle using the backward loop cast-on method and leaving a 10"/25.5cm tail for crocheted button loop, knit first 10 sts of bootie, k2tog to connect sides, knit last 10 sts, then cast on 11 sts using the backward loop cast-on-method—43 sts. Cont in garter st (knit every row) for 7 rows. Bind off knitwise. Cut yarn, leaving a 10"/25.5cm tail for crocheted button loop; do not draw yarn through rem st. Cont as foll:

BUTTON LOOPS
Place rem st on crochet hook, tightly ch 5. Fasten off; do not cut yarn. Use tail to sew end of ch to opposite corner of strap. For second button loop, insert crochet hook into same corner as tail, yo and draw up a loop, tightly ch 5. Cont to work same as opposite strap. Use MC tail to sew center back seam and sole seam. Sew on buttons so straps cross each other. ■

Gauge
24 sts and 48 rows to 4"/10cm over garter st using size 4 (3.5mm) circular needle. *Take time to check gauge.*

Cupcake Cap

Sugar and spice and everything nice—that's what little girls are made of!
Top her off with this cute confectionary hat.

DESIGNED BY FAITH HALE

Sizes

Instructions are written for size newborn–3 months. Changes for size 6–12 months are in parentheses.

Knitted measurements

Head circumference
14 (16)"/35.5 (40.5)cm
Depth
5³/₄ (7)"/14.5 (17.5)cm

Materials

■ 1 3¹/₂oz/100g ball (approx 220yd/201m) of Cascade Yarns *220 Superwash* (superwash wool) each in #894 strawberry cream (MC) and #873 extra creme cafe (CC)

■ 10"/25.5cm scraps of DK or worsted weight yarn in five contrasting colors (for sprinkles)

■ One set (5) size 6 (4mm) double-pointed needles (dpns) *or size to obtain gauge*

■ Stitch marker

Stitch glossary

kf&b Knit in front and back of st— 1 st increased.

Hat

With CC, cast on 72 (80) sts, dividing sts evenly over 4 needles. Join and pm, taking care not to twist sts on needles. Work in k2, p2 rib for 1¹/₂"/4cm. Change to MC.
Next (inc) rnd *K5 (4), kf&b; rep from * around—84 (96) sts. Cont in reverse St st (purl every rnd) until piece measures 4¹/₂ (5¹/₂)"/11.5 (14)cm from beg.

CROWN SHAPING

Dec rnd 1 *P2tog, p 5 (6); rep from * around—72 (84) sts. Purl next rnd.
Dec rnd 2 *P2tog, p 4 (5); rep from * around—60 (72) sts. Purl next rnd.
Dec rnd 3 *P2tog, p 3 (4); rep from * around—48 (60) sts. Purl next rnd.
Dec rnd 4 *P2tog, p 2 (3); rep from * around—36 (48) sts. Purl next rnd.
Dec rnd 5 *P2tog, p 1 (2); rep from * around—24 (36) sts. Purl next rnd.

FOR 6–12 MONTHS SIZE ONLY

Dec rnd 6 *P2tog, p1; rep from * around—24 sts. Purl next rnd.

FOR BOTH SIZES

Last dec rnd [P2tog] 12 times—12 sts. Cut yarn, leaving an 8"/20.5cm tail, and thread through rem sts. Pull tog tightly and secure end.

Finishing

Referring to photo, embroider straight-stitch "sprinkles" over top third of hat using all five colors of scrap yarn. ■

Gauge

24 sts and 30 rnds to 4"/10cm over St st using size 6 (4mm) dpns.
Take time to check gauge.

Slip Stitch Blanket

Slip stitches make for a dense, warm afghan. Multiple colors make it extra-vibrant!

DESIGNED BY LINDA MEDINA

INTERMEDIATE

Knitted measurements
Approx 26" x 29"/66cm x 73.5cm

Materials
- 3 3½ oz/100g balls (each approx 220yd/201m) of Cascade Yarns *220 Superwash* (superwash wool) in #904 colonial blue heather (MC)
- 1 ball each in #821 daffodil (A), #802 green apple (B) and #849 dark aqua (C)
- Size 7 (4.5mm) circular needle, 36"/91cm length *or size to obtain gauge*

Notes
1) Slip all slip stitches purlwise.
2) Carry colors not in use loosely up side edge.

Slip stitch pattern
(over a multiple of 4 sts plus 3)
Row 1 (RS) With A, k3, *sl 1 wyib, k3; rep from * across.
Row 2 With A, k3, *sl 1 wyif, k3; rep from * across.
Row 3 With MC, k1, sl 1 wyib, *k3, sl 1 wyib; rep from *, end k1.

Row 4 With MC, p1, sl 1 wyif, *p3, sl 1 wyif; rep from *, end p1.
Rows 5 and 6 With B, rep rows 1 and 2.
Rows 7 and 8 Rep rows 3 and 4.
Rows 9 and 10 With C, rep rows 1 and 2.
Rows 11 and 12 Rep rows 3 and 4.
Rep rows 1–12 for slip st pat.

Blanket
With MC cast on 139 sts. Work in garter st (knit every row) for 6 rows.
Next row (WS) Purl. Cont in slip st pat and rep rows 1–12 twenty-four times. With MC, work in garter st for 6 rows. Bind off all sts knitwise.

Finishing
SIDE BORDERS
With RS facing and MC, pick up and k 143 sts evenly spaced along side edge. Work in garter st (knit every row) for 6 rows. Bind off all sts knitwise. Rep on opposite side edge. Block piece lightly to measurements. ■

Gauge
23 sts and 42 rows to 4"/10cm over slip st pat using size 7 (4.5mm) circular needle.
Take time to check gauge.

60

Bobble Beanie

With cables, colorwork and bobbles, there's no chance for boredom when knitting this playful hat.

DESIGNED BY LEE GANT

EXPERIENCED

Sizes

Instructions are written for newborn–3 months. Changes for size 6–12 months are in parentheses.

Knitted measurements

Head circumference
14 (16)"/35.5 (40.5)cm
Depth
7½ (8)"/19 (20.5)cm (excluding tab)

Materials

■ 1 3½oz/100g ball (approx 220yd/ 201m) of Cascade Yarns *220 Superwash* (superwash wool) each in #1952 blaze (A) and #903 flamingo pink (B)

■ One set (5) size 4 (3.5mm) double-pointed needles (dpns) *or size to obtain gauge*

■ Cable needle (cn)

■ Stitch marker

Note

To work in the rnd, always read charts from right to left.

Stitch glossary

4-st LC Sl next 2 sts to cn and hold to front, k2, k2 from cn.
MB (Make Bobble) [K1, p1] twice in same st, making 4 sts from one; then pass the 3rd, 2nd and first sts over the last st made.

Hat

With A, cast on 84 (96) sts, dividing sts evenly over 4 needles. Join and pm, taking care not to twist sts on needles. Purl 1 rnd. Change to B and knit 1 rnd. Cont with B as foll:

CABLE BAND

Rnds 1 and 2 *K4, p2; rep from * around.
Rnd 3 *4-st LC, p2; rep from * around.
Rnd 4 Rep rnd 1. Rep rnds 1–4 once more, then rnd 1 once.
Next rnd With A, knit.
Next (inc) rnd With A, purl, inc 6 sts evenly spaced around—90 (102) sts.

BEG CHART PAT I

Rnd 1 Work 6-st rep 15 (17) times. Cont to foll chart in this way to rnd 6, then rep rnds 1–6 until piece measures 3¼"/8cm from beg.

Gauge

24 sts and 28 rnds to 4"/10cm over St st using size 4 (3.5mm) dpns.
Take time to check gauge.

Bobble Beanie

60

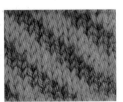

Chart I

6
5
3
1

└─ 6-st rep ─┘

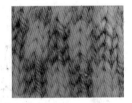

Chart II

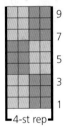

9
7
5
3
1

└─ 4-st rep ─┘

Color Key

- Blaze (A)
- Flamingo Pink (B)

BOBBLE BAND

Rnd 1 With B, knit.
Rnd 2 With B, purl.
Rnds 3 and 4 With B, knit.
Rnd 5 K3 with B, MB with A, *k5 with B, MB with A; rep from * around, end k2 with B.
Rnd 6 With B, knit.
Rnd 7 With B, purl.
Rnd 8 With A, knit.
Rnd (dec) 9 With A, purl, dec 2 sts evenly spaced around—88 (100) sts.

BEG CHART PAT II

Rnd 1 Work 4-st rep 22 (25) times. Cont to foll chart in this way to rnd 9. Cut A. Cont with B as foll:

CROWN SHAPING

Dec rnd 1 *K 6 (8), k2tog; rep from * around—77 (90) sts. Knit next rnd.
Dec rnd 2 *K 5 (7), k2tog; rep from * around—66 (80) sts. Knit next rnd.
Dec rnd 3 *K 4 (6), k2tog; rep from * around—55 (70) sts. Knit next rnd.
Dec rnd 4 *K 3 (5), k2tog; rep from * around—44 (60) sts. Knit next rnd.
Dec rnd 5 *K 2 (4), k2tog; rep from * around—33 (50) sts. Knit next rnd.
Dec rnd 6 *K 1 (3), k2tog; rep from * around—22 (40) sts. Knit next rnd.

FOR NEWBORN–3 MONTHS SIZE ONLY

Dec rnd 7 [K2tog] 11 times—11 sts.
Dec rnd 8 [K2tog] 5 times, k1—6 sts.

FOR 6–12 MONTHS SIZE ONLY

Dec rnd 7 *K2, k2tog; rep from * around—30 sts. Knit next rnd.
Dec rnd 8 *K1, k2tog; rep from * around—20 sts. Knit next rnd.
Dec rnd 9 [K2tog] 10 times—10 sts.
Dec rnd 8 [K2tog, k3] twice—8 sts.

FOR BOTH SIZES

TAB

Rnd 1 With A, knit.
Rnd 2 With B, knit. Rep these 2 rnds 3 (4) times more. Cut B, leaving an 8"/20.5cm tail, and thread through rem sts. Pull tog tightly and secure end. ■